Anchorage

St Jean Vianney △

San Francisco

Managua

△ Yungay

itsunday
nds

isbane

rt

≋ Flood
▲ Bushfire
△ Landslide
⌒ Avalanche

NATURAL DISASTERS

'Flood, fire, tempest, earthquake and acts of God', says the insurance policy. Despite the advance of science and technology, man remains prey to the destructive forces of nature.

What are these forces? What are their effects? Why do they occur? Can they be predicted, prepared for and prevented?

This book discusses the scientific explanations of various natural disasters and their effect on the human and physical environment. Through investigating causes it explores means of prediction, prevention and control.

NATURAL DISASTERS

John E. Butler

HEINEMANN EDUCATIONAL AUSTRALIA

CONTENTS

HEINEMANN EDUCATIONAL AUSTRALIA
85 Abinger Street, Richmond 3121

Copyright © John E. Butler 1976
First Published 1976
Reprinted 1977, 1978 twice

Designed and illustrated by Paulene Raphael.
Printed in Singapore by
Kyodo-Shing Loong Printing Industries Pte Ltd

National Library of Australia cataloguing-in-
publication data:
Butler, John
    Natural disasters.
    Bibliography.
    ISBN 0 85859 126 x.
    I. Disasters — text-books. 1. Title.
    614.875

First Published in Great Britain 1978 by
Heinemann Educational Books Ltd
48 Charles Street, London WIX 8AH

ISBN O 435 34068 9

PREFACE

Most people are fascinated by disasters. Newspapers feature them, television records them and people discuss them. But usually they are treated like other news and quickly forgotten.

This book attempts to develop this interest in a systematic way: disasters are described, reasons are given and the aftermaths are discussed. The reader can consider the scientific background and the social and ecological effects of disasters. He can also simulate and experiment with disaster situations and gain more personal appreciation of them. The plans for disaster relief and prevention can be read and criticized.

All of this leads the reader to consider more than facts. He can see what leads to situations of human conflict and distress, he can appreciate the awesome forces of the earth, he can understand the feelings of the victims and the relief teams, and he can make up his own mind on policies for disaster prevention. Thus the reader develops his own set of values and opinions based on as vivid an understanding as is possible from a book.

I would like to thank the following for their invaluable help in the preparation of this book: Mr Richard Parham of Salisbury College of Advanced Education, for his help with seismology; Mrs Barbara Job for her typing; Mr B. Graham of the Bushfire Research Committee; Professor Gordon MacDonald of the University of Hawaii; Professor G. Melvyn Howe of the University of Strathclyde; Mr Alan Werner of Red Cross Youth; Mrs Ruth Dality of the Natural Disaster Action Committee; Mrs Sheila Walker of the British Consulate-General; and Mr Pro Hart for his generosity in allowing his painting to be used for the cover of the book.

JOHN E. BUTLER

1 EARTHQUAKES

EARTHQUAKE IN CHILE
C. J. Lambert

An extract from the book 'Sweet Waters'

The famous earthquake of 1906 had struck this part of Chile with devastating force, killing thousands of people in Santiago, some fifty miles away, and turning the city into a mass of rubble. On the farm no lives had been lost, but buildings and houses had suffered severely. Everyone was very earthquake-conscious.

They were classed in two categories: the 'Tremblor' or tremor, and the 'Terramoto' or earth render. They seemed to be cumulative, for a slight one every six weeks or so gave us confidence, but as we grew wiser we became more alert than ever if the periods between them extended to some months.

We experienced our first one shortly after our arrival; our feelings were not unlike those we were to enjoy later in air raids during Hitler's war. To begin with, full of fools' confidence, we rather looked down on the locals who were frankly terrified of them, but as soon as we realized what they were capable of doing, we treated them with great respect. Familiarity bred no contempt whatever, and our ears would prick to listen to that first unmistakable sound.

In this part of Chile earthquakes were progressive in their action. First a rapidly approaching rumble like the sound of a half-loaded heavy lorry bounding along a rough road; then a slight shake followed by a pause. Another bigger shake would follow, during which eyes were riveted on the movement of water in a bowl of flowers, or pictures on a wall. Pause and shake continued, reaching a climax and then subsiding at the same tempo, during which everyone sat in a sprinting position ready to make for the safety of open country in a split second of time.

Once and only once did I actually see an earthquake, when Marie and I were riding through a dried-off field, bare of grass. I had dismounted to fix a spur and as I knelt to adjust it I heard that ominous rumble, and looking towards the sound, at that low level I saw a wave coming towards me across the field, just as one travels over the surface of the sea. About one foot in height, it advanced and passed me at great speed, throwing me off balance, while both horses stood with legs splayed out like milking stools to keep their feet. It was a most alarming experience, and I was very frightened indeed. I am very glad I never saw another one; I can feel my hair rising as I write of it.

To show what a lifetime in an earthquake country can do I must tell of an aged relative of my uncle's who had never left her bed in the house for more than eighteen months. One afternoon a particularly vicious quake arrived with far less build-up than usual. The old lady, with seventy years of experience behind her, leapt from her bed, vaulted through the open window and headed the rush for open country and safety. Only when it was all over did she collapse and have to be carried back to bed.

Acknowledgement: the Literary Estate of C. J. Lambert and Chatto & Windus Ltd for this extract from *Sweet Waters*.
Fig 1.0 Meckering earthquake, Western Australia. (Photo: W.A. Newspapers Ltd) ►

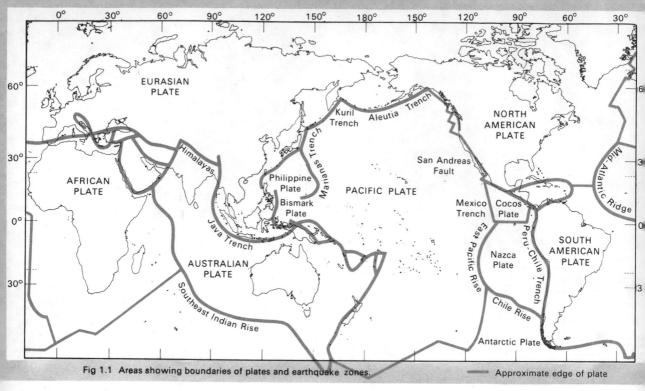

Fig 1.1 Areas showing boundaries of plates and earthquake zones.   ——— Approximate edge of plate

Why they occur

The crust of the earth is in a state of continual change, although most of the changes are very slow. There is a balance between the wearing down of the earth's surface by erosion, and uplift by *tectonic* processes. Tectonic action is the result of forces from within the earth moving the earth's crust. The changes in pressure between the interior of the earth and the crust may cause volcanic action, folding and faulting. These are called *orogenic* (that is, 'mountain-building') processes.

Geologists have been fascinated by the similarities in distribution of earthquakes and volcanoes throughout the world. They have also studied the theory of drifting continents proposed fifty years ago by Alfred Wegener. Recently, geology has adopted the concept of 'plate tectonics' which is closely related to this. The crust of the earth is said to be divided into a number of plates, which are rigid and move slowly. The regions of earthquakes correspond closely with the boundaries of the plates (fig 1.1). Because the plates are moving in different directions, the boundaries are unstable areas. Some plates move sideways, past one another, as in the San Andreas Fault in California (this is called a *transform fault*). In other areas plates moving together force upward

huge mountain ranges such as the Himalayas. In the middle of the Atlantic, the plates moved away from each other, and new rock material has emerged in the gap. This has created the mid-Atlantic ridge.

Although most of the changes along plate boundaries occur over millions of years, there are occasional sudden movements. These may occur if pressure which has built up is suddenly released, allowing movement of part of the crust. Movement of this kind along a fault line causes

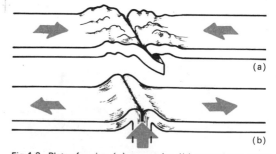

Fig 1.2 Plates forming (a) mountains (b) an undersea ridge.

Fig 1.3 Transform fault.

vibrations which are experienced on the earth's surface as an earthquake. Sometimes an earthquake may be centred quite deeply in the crust and at other times its focus point may be very shallow. The magnitude of an earthquake depends on its depth of origin and the amount of movement of the rocks. The examples of earthquakes discussed later in this chapter show a number of different kinds of occurrences.

Earthquake waves

The effects of earthquakes are felt over wide areas as a result of shock waves spreading out through the crust. These waves are of several types.

1 **Body waves** travel through the interior of the crust. There are two types:

(a) *Primary (P) waves* cause the rock in the crust of the earth to move back and forth in the direction of movement of the waves, creating *pressure* differences.

(b) *Secondary (S) waves* cause the rock to *shear* back and forth at right angles to the direction in which the wave is travelling.

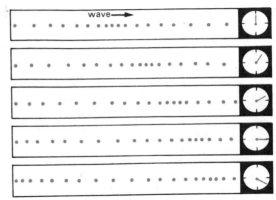

Fig 1.4 Passage of Primary (*P*) wave through rock.

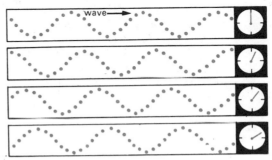

Fig 1.5 Passage of Secondary (*S*) wave through rock.

Fig 1.6 Lateral and vertical movement resulting from the Meckering earthquake. (Photo: W. A. Newspapers Ltd)

Fig 1.7 Effects of the Kanto earthquake, Japan, 1923. (Photo: Japanese National Research Centre for Disaster Prevention)

2 **Surface waves**, as their name implies, travel along the surface of the earth. These are also of two types:

(a) *Rayleigh (R) waves* may be compared to waves on the surface of the sea. A small floating object (and the water itself) is seen to move in a vertical circle as a sea wave passes under it. Rocks on the surface of the earth move in the same way.

(b) *Love (L) waves,* on the other hand, are 'shear' waves on the surface. The rock movement is from side to side, at right angles to the direction of wave movement.

It is the surface waves which cause the most damage in an earthquake. Occasionally *R* waves can be seen when the earth heaves like an ocean wave. Usually, however, the sideways movement of the *L* waves, which rocks and shakes buildings, is the most destructive.

direction of wave ⟶

Fig 1.8 Passage of Rayleigh (*R*) wave through rock.

direction of wave ⟶

Fig 1.9 Passage of Love (*L*) wave through rock.

Recording earthquakes

The instrument which has been developed for recording earthquakes is the *seismograph*. The principle of the seismograph is that a large mass hanging from a flexible support will resist movement. This property of all stationary bodies to resist movement is called *inertia*. During an earthquake the objects around the large mass move, but the mass's inertia and its suspension by flexible supports tend to keep it stationary. When some method of recording the movement of the earth relative to the mass is provided, we have a primitive form of seismograph. The relative movements of the earth and the supported mass are recorded as waves on a line drawn on a moving record sheet.

Refinements to the basic principles of the seismograph have included the use of mirrors and light-sensitive photographic paper for recording, and the damping of the vibrations by oil and magnets. In modern seismometers the 'heavy mass' may be only a tiny cylinder. The small vibrations recorded can be magnified so that they can be read clearly.

■ ACTIVITY

Construct a primitive seismograph using a large mass suspended by wire and a hinge. A recording pen will need to be attached to it so that some record of movement can be made on a sheet of card.

Experiment with the instrument by placing it on a wooden floor or table. Thump the table or floor near the seismograph and record the effects.

An old turntable from a record player can be added to the instrument to move the recording card evenly past the pen.

Fig 1.10 Simple seismographs for recording (a) horizontal movement and (b) vertical movement.

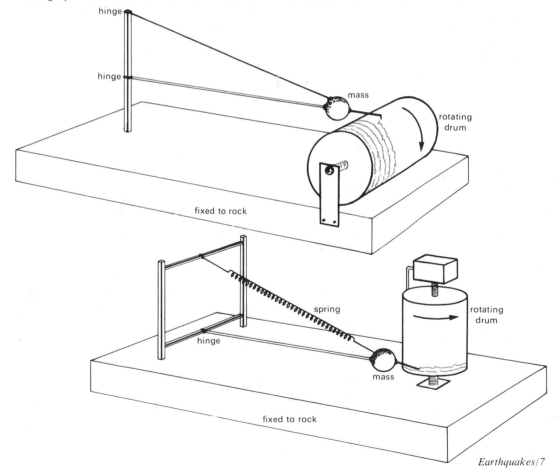

Magnitude and intensity

It is common to see an earthquake described by a figure on a scale giving its *intensity* or its *magnitude*. These are quite distinct measurements but are sometimes confused.

Magnitude

The *magnitude* is the total amount of energy released by the earthquake. The most widely used magnitude scale is the *Richter scale,* which ranges from 0 to 8.9. An earthquake of magnitude 3.0 is ten times greater than one of 2.0, and one of 6.0 would be 10 000 times greater than one of magnitude 2.0. Each increase in a whole number on the scale means an increase of ten times the magnitude. The amount of energy released rises at an even steeper rate than this.

Richter himself has tabulated the average number of earthquakes of various magnitudes for each year. The large number of earthquakes and tremors at small magnitudes is shown clearly.

- Magnitude 4.0 to 4.9
- Magnitude 5.0 to 5.9
- Magnitude greater than 5.9

Fig 1.11 Location of earthquakes in Australia in recent years.

Richter scale

Magnitude range	Number of shocks in a ten-year period
7.75 — 8.6	22
7.0 — 7.7	170
6.0 — 6.9	1,080
5.0 — 5.9	8,000
4.0 — 4.9	62,000
3.0 — 3.9	490,000
2.5 — 2.9	1,000,000

Intensity

The *intensity* of an earthquake is a value reflecting the effect produced. This of course will vary from place to place. Thus, although there can be only one magnitude value, there can be any number of different intensities recorded during an earthquake.

The intensity value is worked out by an observer of an earthquake from the behaviour of objects around him. The most commonly used intensity scale is the modified *Mercalli* scale.

Modified Mercalli scale

I	IMPERCEPTIBLE	Detected only by instruments.
II	VERY WEAK	Detected by sensitive people at rest.
III	WEAK	Loose objects may be disturbed slightly.
IV	MODERATE	Rattling of doors and windows; some sleepers awake.
V	FAIRLY STRONG	Most sleepers awake; noticed out of doors; bells ring.
VI	STRONG	Furniture overthrown; cracking of plaster.
VII	VERY STRONG	Some damage to buildings.
VIII	DESTRUCTIVE	Walls crack; chimneys fall.
IX	VERY DESTRUCTIVE	Severe damage; some buildings destroyed.
X	DEVASTATING	Foundations, roads, pipes etc. damaged.
XI	CATASTROPHIC	Few buildings survive; fissures in ground.
XII	MAJOR CATASTROPHE	Complete destruction; crumpling of ground.

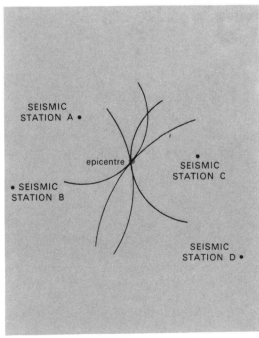

Locating earthquakes

Physicists have studied these *seismic* waves which spread out from a disturbance of the earth's crust and have sorted them into different groups (see page 5 and 6). Seismographs at a distance from an earthquake can record the arrival of each of the different kinds of wave movement from the source of the earthquake.

First to arrive are the *primary (P) waves* which move more quickly than the others. The *secondary (S) waves* move at about two-thirds the velocity of the primary waves. Both P and S waves move directly through the interior of the earth from the *focus* (point of origin) of the earthquake. Moving more slowly than P and S waves are the *surface waves*. These spread out across the earth's surface and reach distant places much later than P and S waves.

Seismologists use the P and S waves to establish the location of an earthquake. The seismic records of a station show the separate arrival times of the P and S waves. Because the time difference increases with distance from the earthquake, seismologists can calculate the distance of any recorded earthquake from the seismic station. A circle of equivalent radius to that distance can be drawn on a map, as can the calculated distances of the earthquake from other stations. The point at which the arcs intersect is the *epicentre* of the earthquake. The epicentre is the point on the earth's surface directly above the focus of the earthquake. Sometimes the focus is quite shallow and near the epicentre, but at other times it is much deeper.

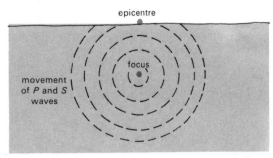

Fig 1.12 Focus and epicentre.

Fig 1.13 Locating the epicentre.

San Francisco . . .

WHOLESALE DIST. BURNING
M. APR/8 '06

At 5.12 a.m., on Wednesday 18 April 1906, the San Andreas fault line reacted to the great pressures which had been built up on each side, and slipped. Along the almost straight line of the fault the countryside was ripped. Roads were displaced, belts of trees moved, buildings were demolished and ships above the fault-line in the sea appeared to have hit an object below.

But it was the spread of the seismic waves which hit San Francisco that were most significant. The first waves hit the city and set it shaking, bringing down walls, towers and whole houses. Then there was a gap of ten seconds before the second phase brought more buildings tumbling, as well as breaking water pipes and gas pipes, and heaving up roads into impassable rubble heaps.

In the first seventeen minutes after the earthquake, fifty fires were reported in the city, but the Fire Department could do little. When fire trucks reached the fires they found that there was no water in the mains — the earthquake

Fig 1.14 San Francisco 1906: fire after earthquake. (Photo: Advertiser Newspapers Ltd)

had split pipes leading from Crystal Springs and San Andreas Lakes.

The fires quickly spread through the many wooden buildings of the city, and other new fires started. One such fire, which has come to be known as the 'ham-and-eggs fire', started when a woman lit a fire in her stove. The fire spread to the wooden walls through an earthquake-damaged flue. The pattern of the spread of fires is shown in the map.

In the early hours of the fires the military assumed command without the approval of the Mayor. Acting on their own initiative, soldiers shot looters without trial. Later, the groups of soldiers were reported to have shot people who did not immediately obey a shouted order. The military also decided that the only way to stop the fires was to dynamite buildings in their path, to create open spaces across which the fires could not jump. However, the first attempts at this using black powder, the only explosive available, sent burning debris flying across the street starting a new fire in Chinatown. When dynamite was available it was used inexpertly, without checks on the wind direction or the path of the fire. When the dynamite supply was exhausted, some soldiers started their own fires in buildings, which inevitably joined the general inferno. Eventually an effective dynamite line was set up on the west side of Van Ness Avenue (see fig 1.15) which held the fire, but this was not until the second day.

As fires still raged, a new problem appeared in parts of the city on the third day — corpses — bodies of people crushed, burned and shot. An attempt was made to bury them, but there was no lime or disinfectant to help the burial squads. Rats were appearing in large numbers as they found their way easily in and out of the broken sewers.

It took until 7.15 a.m. Saturday, over three days since the earthquake, for the fire to be put out. During its raging progress over the city it had been aided by strong winds, careless dynamiting, arson by some soldiers, and the unavailability of water from the city's broken pipes. It had not been until late on the Thursday that the Navy and Marines were able to help by providing two fireboats and a water tender to carry water from the bay. Later one of the main pipelines was repaired, a major step in bringing the fire under control.

The story of the San Francisco earthquake has been well documented. Try to read one of the books written about it or see the film 'San Francisco'. Some writers have called it the most studied earthquake in history. Certainly the research into the possibility of future earthquakes in the San Francisco area has been extensive.

The personalities involved in the San Francisco earthquake have also been studied and written about. The mayor of the city, Eugene Schmitz, was seen as a hero by some inhabitants; later, however, he was shown to be a puppet of Abraham Ruef, a powerful underworld figure. The character of General Funston, the impetuous soldier who took command of the city without authority, is an interesting contrast with that of Dr Devine,

Fig 1.15 Extent of the San Francisco fire.

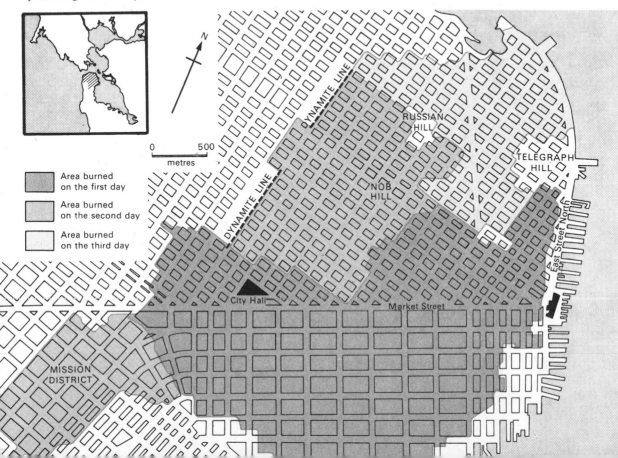

Area burned on the first day

Area burned on the second day

Area burned on the third day

the first disaster relief worker for the Red Cross. Also, the famous Italian tenor, Enrico Caruso, happened to be in San Francisco at the time of the earthquake. The stories of all these people make interesting reading.

■ DISCUSSION

1 Why did the fire spread? Why was dynamite used by soldiers? What problems can you see in its use?
2 What human factors contributed to the San Francisco disaster?
3 For many years after 1906, San Franciscans called the disaster the 'San Francisco Fire'. Little mention was made of the earthquake. Why do you think people reacted in this way?

... the future

The San Andreas fault runs through the area of San Francisco. This is a *transform fault* between two huge plates or sections of the earth's crust. The two plates have pressure on them to move in opposite directions, resulting in an average movement of 6 cm a year. But the movement is not smooth or constant. If it were, there would be little danger of disaster.

The fault is not a single straight line, but a collection of closely spaced lines of weakness. In reaction to the opposing pressures from each plate there is a build up of pressure, and then release. It is the release of pressure with the accompanying sudden movement which causes seismic waves. This is what happened in 1906. The pressure had built up so much that the move-

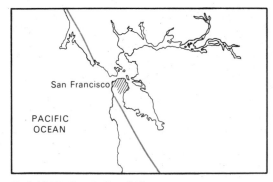

Fig 1.16 The San Andreas fault.

ment and the resulting seismic waves were very large indeed.

Although Californian researchers have studied the San Andreas fault very closely, the timing of the movements is still unpredictable. In 1971 a movement of a nearby fault line through Los Angeles caused great damage.

Predictions have been made that San Francisco will soon suffer another earthquake comparable with the 1906 disaster. But estimates of 50 000 dead and damage of $50 000 million have not deterred people from living in San Francisco. In fact, the inhabitants are casual about possible danger. Many of the city's hospitals and emergency provisions lie along the fault line and would be wrecked in any major earthquake.

Some areas of new suburban housing, near the San Andreas fault line, are built on clay which is quite firm under normal conditions. However, laboratory experiments have shown that water particles within it will spread equally among the clay particles when the whole area vibrates. This makes the firm clay into a soup-like material which will not support any weight and will flow down a slope. Houses will sink into the material or be carried with it (see page 15). Laboratory experiments and actual slides in Quebec, Japan and Norway have shown that it is possible. Will the next San Francisco earthquake cause a submergence of some suburbs?

In the National Center for Earthquake Research at Menlo Park near San Francisco a possible way to control the San Andreas Fault has been devised. Experiments have been conducted in which rocks were placed under pressure from different directions. The rocks grind against each other as they would in a real earthquake, jerking and sticking against each other. However when water is pumped into the joints and fractures of the fault line, the surfaces move more easily. Movements are smaller and more frequent. Could this be used in San Francisco? Could the San Andreas fault be made to move in small jerks, under man's control, thus more evenly releasing the pressure which has built up?

A possible scheme is the boring of three holes into the Earth's surface, each 4 km in depth. Water would be pumped from the end holes, thus preventing movement there, and pumped into the middle hole, to allow small, controlled movements. With a series of 500 boreholes,

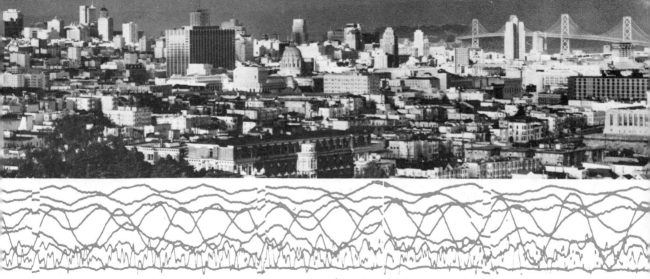

it might be possible to control the pressures built up in the San Andreas Fault. The cost of the project would be about $1 million for each hole and would take ten years to complete.

This method could only be used on fault lines where movement occurs near the surface, and which are self-lubricating at greater depths. Therefore California, Turkey and Iran could use the water-lubrication method, but not Alaska, Japan, Chile and Peru.

Fig 1.17 San Francisco today. The seismogram suggests an uncertain future. (Photo: U.S. Information Service)

■ DISCUSSION

What is the cost of building a new ten-storey building? What would a street of these cost to rebuild if they were destroyed in an earthquake? Compare this with the cost of the water-lubrication boreholes. What other problems can you foresee in the use of the boreholes?

... report on earthquake

In contrast to the previous views on the possible tragedy of a future earthquake in San Francisco, a report prepared after the 1971 Los Angeles earthquake takes a more optimistic view. It says that San Francisco is better prepared now than in 1906, that no general conflagration is likely, and that high-rise buildings are not expected to be destroyed. The Golden Gate and Oakland Bay Bridges were built to withstand earthquakes, but their approaches, like San Francisco airport, are built on Bay mud, and are therefore likely to be put out of action in an earthquake.

The report looked at factors such as time of day and season. The worst combination of factors, at 4.30 p.m. on a week day, would give an estimated death toll of 10 000 with 40 000 casualties. In the most favourable time 2.30 a.m., there would be 2500 dead and 11 000 casualties. Wooden frame houses, which are typical of the suburbs, are largely earthquake-resistant because of their flexibility.

During a future major earthquake there would be general loss of electric power and phone services, but the water system now is designed so that main breaks can be isolated quickly. There are special high-pressure systems to pump water from the Bay to the city centre.

Fire damage would take the homes of 20 000 people, says the report, but the presence of sixteen 'packaged disaster hospitals' in storage around the Bay would be helpful. These could be set up in buildings such as schools and hotels in about six hours.

■ DISCUSSION

Debate the optimistic and pessimistic predictions about the results of a future San Francisco earthquake. Can a large city have a workable plan for a large disaster? What are the difficulties?

■ ACTIVITY

If you get the chance, watch the television documentary 'The City that waits to die', produced by the BBC.

Managua - earthquake and aftermath

Managua, the capital of the Central American republic of Nicaragua, lies between fault lines within a geologically unstable zone. It suffered major earthquakes in 1885 and 1931.

On 23 December 1972, it was hit by an earthquake which measured only 6.3 on the Richter Scale, but which killed 6000 and injured another 20 000. The reason for the pronounced effects of the earthquake was that Managua was on the exact epicentre of a shallow earthquake, and that the rocks underlying the city were compacted volcanic debris. The shocks lasted for two hours, some tremors oscillating horizontally, some vertically. At 12.27 in the morning came 'the killer' which threw people and buildings around. All clocks in the city stopped. The roof of a nine-storey hotel was seen to bounce a metre in the air and come down with a crash. Masonry structures collapsed and the many wooden buildings of the city caught fire.

The central part of the city was left devastated, but the surrounding areas were less affected. The Government, therefore, at first refused to bring food supplies into the city centre, hoping that the people would move out and reduce the chances of a spread of disease. This led to profiteers in the city selling bread at $2 a loaf and water at $2 a bottle. Emergency food flown in by organizations such as CARE piled up at the airport. Rioting and looting were widespread in the city, and shooting broke out between rival groups of looters. At least 32 people were treated for bullet wounds after the earthquake. The Government leader commented that it was not hunger or disease which was the biggest problem in the city, but the looters who were scouring the rubble.

To a small country of two million people, the destruction of a capital city, the loss of millions of dollars worth of buildings and belongings, and the loss of life and injury of thousands, is a traumatic and far-reaching disaster. The Government was forced to rely on strong-arm techniques for reconstruction, overriding the constitutional law. The possible shift of location of the capital was debated, but with little result because of the widespread earthquake risk throughout the region. The country's second city, Leon (population 50 000), also lies in an unstable zone.

The Managuan earthquake illustrates the problem of looting, profiteering and violence which can follow destruction on this scale. With roads impassable, buildings reduced to rubble, and communication lines cut, there is inevitably a period when little can be done to enforce order. The very processes of law rely on a routine, ordered way of life of the people. Thus, the looting and disorder which Managua experienced has been seen as a dramatic example of the human chaos which follows most sudden catastrophes.

Fig 1.18 Managua: soldier grapples with looters. (Photo: UPI)

Niigata - liquefaction following earthquake

Niigata, a city of 340 000 people, is built on a low-lying sandy area at the mouth of the Shinano River on the island of Honshu in Japan.

On 16 June 1964, an earthquake (magnitude 7.7) occurred 70 km out to sea. There were few deaths, but one third of the city subsided, because of *liquefaction* of the sandy material on which the city was built. Ground water rose through the sand and bubbled to the surface. The flooding was worsened by the effects of a high tide and a small tsunami caused by the earthquake. These stopped water from moving down the river, and the city was flooded.

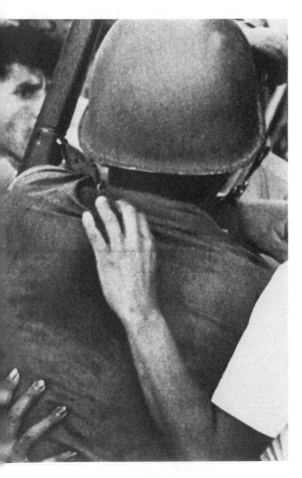

It was the flooding due to liquefaction and the river which caused subsidence of part of the city. Many buildings were not wrecked, but they sank into the saturated soil. Some four-storey apartment buildings tilted to an angle of 40°. Residents were able to walk along the former front wall of the building and get their possessions through the window. Other buildings cracked as they slowly subsided.

Although there was flooding, fire still proved to be a hazard. Seventy tanks of the oil refineries caught fire and destroyed 300 nearby houses.

The earthquake of Niigata demonstrates clearly how the site of a city is an important factor in earthquake damage. The region was considered to be safer than many others in Japan but the events of 1964 made the inhabitants aware of the dangers of the low-lying silty area near the mouth of the river.

Investigation of the causes of subsidence has been done in laboratories. Experiments have shown that in alluvial deposits which are saturated in the lower and middle levels, vibrations can cause the water to rise to the surface, saturating all the alluvium. The loss of friction between silt particles lowers the supporting ability of the material, and buildings sink into the mud. The process has been called *liquefaction*. It seems to occur mostly in areas with thick alluvial deposits susceptible to saturation.

Investigations of the San Francisco earthquake of 1906 have found evidence of subsidence craters where the water came to the surface during liquefaction. Large areas of San Francisco are built on Bay mud, a thick silty deposit with a high water content. The nature of the surface rocks on the site of a city is known to be an important factor in the effects of earthquakes. From observations, geologists and earthquake-watchers have noted that buildings built on very solid massive rock are often not damaged so much as those on softer material.

Anchorage

The earthquake with the highest magnitude of recent times was recorded in Alaska on 27 March 1964. Only the low density of population prevented the death toll from rising to higher than 154. The magnitude on the Richter scale was recorded at 8.7, and *tsunamis* (see p. 36) set off by the quake reached the coast of California, drowning eighteen people.

Geologists who investigated the area afterwards were amazed by some of the effects of the earthquake. In one area a mountain had split into two parts. One side of it, including its summit, plunged downwards, flying over a 150 metre ridge as if it were a ski-jump, not touching vegetation on the far side of the ridge.

The falling mountainside then apparently spread out like a flying carpet as it disintegrated. Beneath it there must have been a cushion of compressed air, so that it travelled like a huge hovercraft at more than 170 km/h. The carpet of rock fragments was over 1 km wide and 2 km long. After travelling over the almost flat glacier surface without touching it, the rock landed on a lower portion of the Sherman glacier.

Evidence for this almost incredible event lies in the discovery by geologists that snow and ice on the glacier were undisturbed. If the rock had slid along the glacier, the friction would have left obvious marks. This remarkable landslide shows not only the awesome power of the earthquake but the strange events which can happen on such a huge scale.

Agadir -
disease following an earthquake

In February 1960, 12 000 people were killed when the Moroccan city of Agadir was destroyed by earthquake. The city was almost flattened into a mass of rubble, containing the bodies of thousands of people.

After the first few days of rescue operations, the immediate problem became the prevention of disease spreading from the decaying corpses to the people who had survived, and possibly to other areas.

The city was declared a 'closed city' — officially no one was allowed in, but it was difficult to stop former inhabitants searching for possessions and friends. The survivors were housed in a tent city, 10 km away.

A few days after the earthquake, rats were seen to be rife among the ruins and rabid dogs appeared. Troops reported shooting jackals which were digging in the rubble for bodies. Proposals

Fig 1.19 Thousands were buried in the rubble of Agadir, 1960. (Photo: UPI)

Are earthquakes and nuclear explosions linked?

Since the end of World War II, nations have been experimenting with nuclear power. There has often been speculation on whether a powerful nuclear explosion could cause an earthquake. Underground nuclear explosions, in particular, have been suspected of causing changes in the pressure of rocks which could lead to other earth movements.

The advocates of this theory point to the 1959 earthquake in Iran which had been preceded by an underground nuclear explosion in the Western Hemisphere, an earthquake in Turkey following an explosion in Nevada, and the June 1960 earthquake in Peru following a French hydrogen bomb test in the Pacific.

Opponents say that occurrences such as these are coincidences, and that the distances between the explosion and the earthquake in these cases is too great.

However, there seems no doubt that, on a small scale, nuclear explosions can cause earth tremors. In Nevada, in 1968, a 1.2 megaton bomb detonated underground, was followed by thirty tremors within three days. The site of the explosion was an old fault line which was probably reactivated.

Obviously, international politics become important where there is a possible link between nuclear tests in one country and earthquakes in another. Already diplomatic protests have been made from Peru to the French, and from Japan to the U.S.A., concerning the effects of nuclear tests on earthquakes in their own region.

■ ACTIVITY

1 Keep a record of earthquakes from newspapers. See if there are any comments on links with nuclear explosions.
2 Discuss the possible use of nuclear explosions to trigger earthquakes as a destructive war weapon.

were made to eliminate the spread of disease. They first proposed the use of napalm to burn out the decaying matter, but this was rejected by the local people who were Muslim. Muslim religion forbids the burning of bodies.

Therefore it was decided to spread quicklime over the ruins, which became the job of many of the medical personnel, and to spray chemical disinfectant from helicopters. After this, there were mass burials where possible, and bulldozers were used to level the rubble of the city.

A site for a new city was chosen some distance away from the old city. But there was soon building activity on the rubble — people who owned land there were, of course, reluctant to give it up. Others had houses undamaged on the edge of the city. The process of shifting the site of the city proved to be no easy task.

■ ACTIVITY

1 What other health problems might occur in the aftermath of an earthquake?
2 Argue for and against the idea of shifting the site of a city hit by an earthquake.

Earthquake - resistant buildings

The buildings which cause most deaths in earthquakes are those built from bricks and masonry. If the walls sway they quickly break, bringing the roof and upper floors down on the occupants.

The only possible earthquake-resistant building would be an expensive steel box structure. However, structures with a framework which can move are suitable for earthquake areas. Wood-frame structures and modern, steel-girder skyscrapers can vibrate with the earthquake without disintegrating.

The buildings in Tokyo in 1923 were mostly wooden. In the earthquake that year they resisted the vibrations, but were destroyed in the ensuing fires. Tokyo now has streets of buildings which conform to height restrictions (see fig 1.20). This gives the city a uniformity which is unlike that of other modern cities. However, in recent years there has been a relaxation of the height restrictions and a number of large hotels have sprung up, apparently still with earthquake resistance.

Frank Lloyd Wright, the famous American architect, designed the old Imperial Hotel in Tokyo during World War I. It was to be earthquake-proof, low and squat, and it resisted successfully the 1923 earthquake. Even the large ornamental pool was functional in the aftermath of the disaster, providing water to quench the fires.

Fig 1.20 Tokyo's central business district today.
(Photo: author)

2 VOLCANOES

VESUVIUS A.D. 79

An extract from
'The Letters of the Younger Pliny'

My uncle was stationed at Misenum, in active command of the fleet. On 24 August, in the early afternoon, my mother drew his attention to a cloud of unusual size and appearance ... It was not clear at that distance from which mountain the cloud was rising (it was afterwards known to be Vesuvius); its general appearance can best be expressed as being like an umbrella pine, for it rose to a great height on a sort of trunk and then split off into branches, I imagine because it was thrust upwards by the first blast and then left unsupported as the pressure subsided, or else it was borne down by its own weight so that it spread out and gradually dispersed. Sometimes it looked white, sometimes blotched and dirty, according to the amount of soil and ashes it carried with it. My uncle's scholarly acumen saw at once that it was important enough for a closer inspection, and he ordered a boat to be made ready, telling me I could come with him if I wished. I replied that I preferred to go on with my studies ...

By dawn the light was still dim and faint. The buildings round us were already tottering, and the open space we were in was too small for us not to be in real and imminent danger if the house collapsed. This finally decided us to leave the town. We were followed by a panic-stricken mob of people wanting to act on someone else's decision in preference to their own, who hurried us on our way by pressing hard behind in a dense crowd ... The carriages we had ordered to be brought out began to run in different directions though the ground was quite level, and would not remain stationary even when wedged with stones. We also saw the sea sucked away and apparently forced back by the earthquake: at any rate it receded from the shore so that quantities of sea creatures were left stranded on dry sand. On the landward side a fearful black cloud was rent by forked and quivering bursts of flame, and parted to reveal great tongues of fire, like flashes of lightning magnified in size.

Soon afterwards the cloud sank down to earth and covered the sea; it had already blotted out Capri and hidden the promontory of Misenum from sight ... Ashes were already falling, not as yet very thickly. I looked round: a dense black cloud was coming up behind us, spreading over the earth like a flood ... We had scarcely sat down to rest when darkness fell, not the dark of a moonless or cloudy night, but as if the lamp had been put out in a closed room. You could hear the shrieks of women, the wailing of infants, and the shouting of men; some were calling their parents, others their children or their wives, trying to recognize them by their voices.

At last the darkness thinned and dispersed into smoke or cloud; then there was genuine daylight, and the sun actually shone out, but yellowish as it is during an eclipse. We were terrified to see everything changed, buried deep in ashes like snowdrifts.

Fig 2.0 Vesuvius in eruption. (Photo: Advertiser Newspapers Ltd)

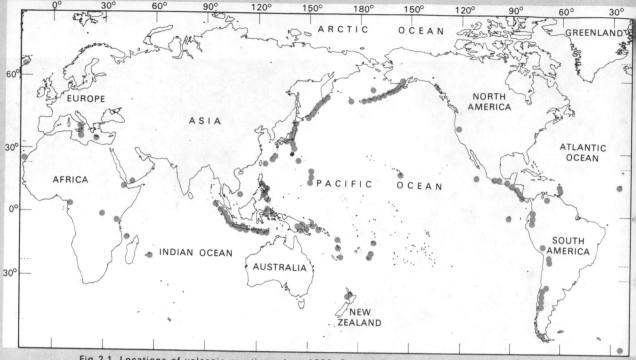

Fig 2.1 Locations of volcanic eruptions since 1900. Compare Fig 1.1.

Volcanic explosions

The *active* volcanoes of the world are shown in fig 2.1. Compare this map with that showing areas of recent mountain building. In the areas shown on both the maps, the earth's crust has been under tremendous pressure from colliding plates (see page 4). The crust has buckled and folded, raising belts of mountains such as the Andes. During the period of folding there would have been much volcanic activity through breaks in the crust. At the present time some of these volcanoes continue to erupt, while others are *extinct* or *dormant*.

The construction of a composite volcano is explained on page 24. A distinction is made between the *lava flows* and the *tephra* (thrown-out broken material, either solid or liquid) from a volcano. To study the destructive and constructive effects of volcanoes it is necessary to look at these in more detail.

Lava flows

Two of the most common types of lava flows are known by their Hawiian names — *Pahoehoe* and *Aa* (pronounced *Pa-hoyee-hoyee* and *Ah-ah*).

Pahoehoe flows have a smooth crust, often containing rolling hills and hollows. In some places the dragging and twisting of the crust has caused a folded surface which looks like coils of rope. The solidifying of the crust can stop the flows fairly quickly.

Aa flows have a much rougher surface, sometimes with masses of spines and broken fragments. In general Aa flows advance slowly (10 to 100 m/h).

Fig 2.2. An advancing *Aa* lava flow after a volcanic eruption in Hawaii, 1955. (Photo: U.S. Geological Survey)

Pieces from the front of the flow continually break off and fall beneath the advancing front.

Fragmental flows

These differ from lava flows in that the material deposited is similar to that from a volcanic explosion — fragments of rocks and ash. They move at great speed and over great distances and thus can be the most destructive agents of volcanoes.

Glowing avalanches

These are avalanches of incandescent rock fragments mixed with hot air and accompanied by a huge cloud of dust and ash. They move down valleys at speeds up to 150 km/h, and strike anything in their path with tremendous force. The fragments of glowing rock continue to give off gas as the avalanche moves, which keeps the whole avalanche in a state similar to a continuous explosion. Sometimes the cloud of dust, ash and very hot air may separate from the path of the avalanche and cause destruction by itself. This was what destroyed the town of St Pierre, in the French West Indies, and its 30 000 people in 1902. An avalanche of hot ash was responsible for much of the destruction around Vesuvius in A.D. 64.

Volcanic mudflows

These have probably destroyed more property than any other type of volcanic action. They consist of a mixture of volcanic ash, soil and water which can travel down a hillside at a speed of 20 km/h. The source of the water is varied, but it can come from a crater lake, rapid melting of snow on the volcano, heavy rains, or the movement of glowing avalanches into streams. Sometimes the vibrations of the erupting volcano

Fig 2.3 A lava river, Hawaii, 1955. (Photo: U.S. Geological Survey)

are enough to shift water-saturated material on the slopes.

Ashflows

These can cover an extensive area around a volcano. They consist of fine pieces of material of sand-or dust-size, and move down the slopes of the volcano, depositing themselves at the base. Like the glowing avalanches, the ashflows contain gas which acts as a cushion and helps to carry them over large distances.

These are some of the products of a volcanic explosion which can cause destruction. There are still other kinds of flows and explosions which are not described here. Obviously, it is not a simple matter to protect people and property from volcanoes when the destructive agents are so diverse.

A composite volcano

When pressure in the *magma reservoir* is great enough, the plug of solid material in the crater breaks, and the volcano erupts.

The cone is often built up by a sequence of explosions of tephra and lava flows. Cracks in the tephra often fill with molten lava. This leads to the characteristic *sills* and *dykes* (horizontal and vertical seams of hard rock) among the softer tephra. Smaller *lateral cones* may form at the outlet of a dyke.

The shape of a volcano cone varies from place to place, depending on the eruptions. Sometimes an eruption will break out of the side of a cone, altering the shape. In some cases there are few explosions of tephra, and the continuous lava flow forms a broad, low dome, called a *shield volcano*.

■ ACTIVITY

1 By looking into books on physical geology or geomorphology, find out what the sills, dykes, cones and other volcanic features look like after many thousands of years of erosion.

2 Make a model of a volcano, labelling all parts clearly.

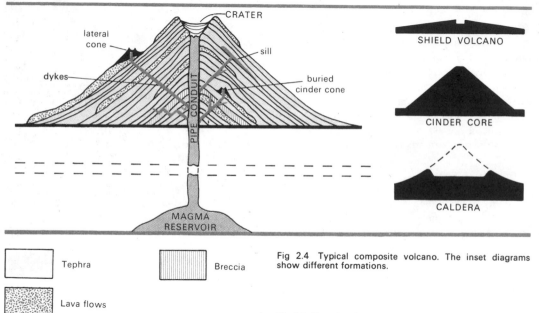

Tephra

Breccia

Lava flows

Fig 2.4 Typical composite volcano. The inset diagrams show different formations.

Fig 2.5 Vesuvius dormant.

Vesuvius

Three cities were destroyed in the eruption described by Pliny the Younger — Pompeii, Herculaneum and Stabiae. Pompeii and Stabiae were buried by tephra. The layers of tephra piled up on one another, as shown in the diagram (fig 2.7).

The layers of deposits shown in the diagram were discovered by excavations in Pompeii during this century. Most of the lower layers of pumice material came from the magma which had blocked the vent of the volcano and caused the explosion. The *lapilli* (small stones thrown out) came from the sides of the cone which was blown up in succeeding explosions. Ash was also deposited in layers from these explosions. The first explosion of Vesuvius described by Pliny on page 20, produced the pumice material which buried Pompeii to a depth of 2.5 metres.

Fig 2.6 Red hot lava from Vesuvius enters a village street, 1944. (Photo: Advertiser Newspapers Ltd)

Fig 2.7 Successive layers of tephra bury a house in Pompeii.

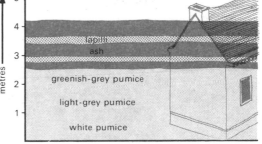

Krakatoa

Krakatoa, although the name of an island, to most people signifies the volcanic explosion of 1883. It has been described as one of the greatest explosions and loudest noises of all time. Its effects on people were not in the immediate area of the island but on a widespread region throughout South-East Asia.

Krakatoa had erupted in 1680 but was dormant until 1883. During that year, from May to August there were a series of explosions which could be heard on Java, 160 km away. Smoke poured from the vent, and the air was thick with dust and sulphurous fumes. On August 26th a much larger explosion, followed by others, began the final phase of the eruption. The cloud rising from Krakatoa reached an altitude of about 25 km and lightning continually flashed through it. The thunderous noise of continual eruption could be heard all night in Batavia (now Jakarta), Java.

Continuous eruption for nineteen hours poured huge amounts of material from the magma chamber, and left the island like the roof of an empty cave. At 10 a.m. on the 27th, 25 km of the island (about three quarters of its area), collapsed. The sea poured into the cavern of molten rocks. Water evaporated into great clouds of steam and the whole island exploded with one huge roar. It sent rocks, dust and steam into the air in a massive cloud of hot air. A wall of water was hurled outwards from the explosion. The roar of the destruction of Krakatoa was heard 5000 km away.

The tsunami created by the explosion swept across the Sunda Strait at a speed of 480 km/h, and struck the coast of Java and Sumatra. Its height was estimated to be over 30 metres. As it swept across the shallow coasts, it killed over 30 000 people. These were mainly the inhabitants of the fishing villages and the farming villages on the coastal plain. At Port Elizabeth, in South Africa, 8000 km away, ships rocked at anchor as the remnant of the tsunami hit them.

A blast of hot air from the explosion reached as far as Batavia and Buitenzorg (now Jakarta and Bogor). However the noise was heard as far as Australia, New Guinea, the Philippines and India. The dust cloud which had soared into the air spread thick layers of dust on Sumatra and Java and large areas of the Indian Ocean, and finer dust was carried around the earth by upper atmosphere winds. For months afterwards sunsets all over the world were peculiarly brilliant and long lasting. The great heights of the dust allowed sunlight to be reflected long after sundown, and people in all continents saw unusually deep-red skies at twilight.

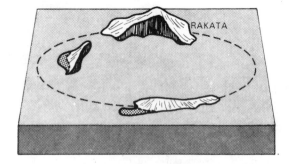

Fig 2.8 Formation of Krakatoa before and after the eruption.

Fig 2.9 The area affected by the Krakatoa explosion. ▶

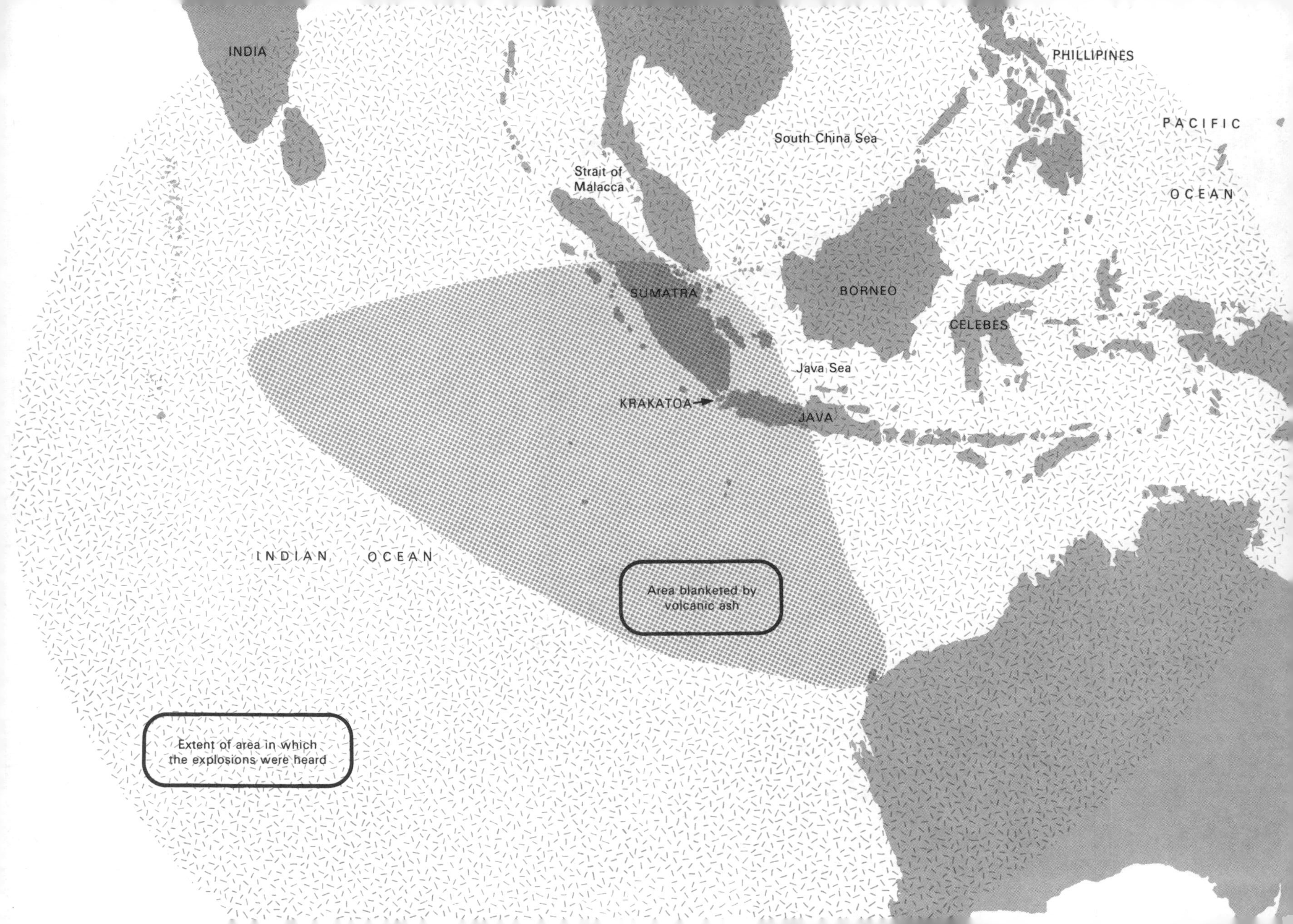

Extent of area in which the explosions were heard

Area blanketed by volcanic ash

INDIA

INDIAN OCEAN

Strait of Malacca

SUMATRA

KRAKATOA

JAVA

Java Sea

South China Sea

BORNEO

CELEBES

PHILLIPINES

PACIFIC OCEAN

Heimaey

On 23 January 1973, on the island of Heimaey, off the south coast of Iceland, the ground quietly split open near the town and a curtain of molten lava was shot into the sky. The split (fig 2.11) was about 1500 metres long but later the eruption centralized at one spot and a new volcano began to form.

Heimaey is the largest island of the Vestmannaeyjar group on the south coast of Iceland. Its population is about 6000, most of whom are engaged in fishing or farming. The cone of an old volcano, Helgafell, dominated the landscape of the island. Examination by using carbon-14 dating methods had shown that the last eruption was 5400 years ago. The new eruption was a shock to the inhabitants who had assumed that all volcanic activity on Heimaey had ceased.

Dangers

The people of the town were in danger from three things. The glowing bombs of molten lava were a constant fire hazard, the heavy tephra fall was blocking roads and piling up on roofs, and the lava flow was creeping close to the town and its harbour.

The tephra fragments were quite light and easily blown by the wind, but fortunately the usual prevailing south-east wind occurred only a couple of times in the first two weeks. Even so, the tephra layer was up to five metres deep in parts of the town. Some houses with flat or gently-sloping roofs collapsed under the weight of tephra. The fish-processing plants were kept in operation by continual clearing of the roofs.

The lava flow surged into the sea and then spread out to the north and south (fig 2.13). Two

Fig 2.10 Aerial view of Heimaey before eruption...

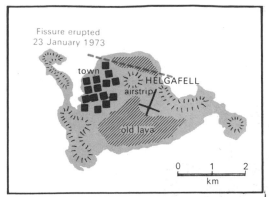

Fig 2.11 The fissure on Heimaey in relation to the town and the airstrip.

dangers were apparent. Lava was moving toward the eastern part of the town, and toward the harbour. To the townspeople who had reversed

...and after, showing radical alteration of coastline.
Fig 2.12 (Photos: Iceland Geodetic Survey)

their original attitude of evacuating and abandoning the town, to one of preservation, the possible loss of the harbour was disastrous.

Prevention methods

Many schemes for stopping the lava before it closed the harbour were put forward. There were suggestions of bombing the crater, but the effects of this were unpredictable. In some areas of the lava flow, the red-hot lava was sprayed with water. The idea was to cool and solidify the lava, forming a wall which might divert the flow. This worked in part but the pressure of flow was too great for successful diversion. A temporary diversion was formed by building a tephra wall in front of the oncoming lava. It was even suggested that the lava flow should be allowed to block the harbour and that a new harbour entrance should be cut through the spit of sand and shingle, or *tombolo*, north of the town.

Effects on the economy

The harbour was particularly important because the island had a fishing fleet of 77 boats and 90 per cent of the workforce of the town were employed in some part of the fishing-industry. A large sale of *capelin* (a fish of the salmon family) had been promised to Japan just before the eruption.

There were several fish-processing plants and five freezing plants in the town, allowing Heimaey to supply almost 20 per cent of Iceland's fish exports. The 800 motor cars for 5300 people were a sign of the island's prosperity.

The season for the capelin catch was to begin in February. The eruption was a major threat to its success. More importantly, the blocking of the harbour by the lava flow would have had such long-term effects on the fishing industry that all possible attempts were made to prevent it.

The position of the electricity cable and freshwater pipe in the harbour presented another danger to the islanders. The island community depended entirely on the mainland for freshwater, electricity and telephone contact.

After the eruptions

The volcano erupted for five months and five days, pouring forth 250 million cubic metres of lava and tephra. The area of Heimaey was increased by 2.5 km² by the spread of the lava flow but fortunately the harbour was not blocked. The

Fig 2.13 Heimaey during eruption. (Photo: Iceland Geodetic Survey)

water supply was interrupted for only a few days, but the electricity cable was severed by underground volcanic activity.

Economically, the island and the whole nation suffered greatly. The loss of the most important weeks of fishing, and the closure of the fish-processing plants resulted in a loss of export income. However, the fishing fleet later operated from the mainland, which also provided houses for the displaced islanders.

By August, families had started to return to the island, to repair their houses and begin normal life again. Over 60 per cent of the original population decided to return to the island. Money was provided from a relief fund. Jobs were available in cleaning-up and reconstruction operations, and later in the fish-processing plants.

A large area of grazing-land was covered by the tephra and lava and the seeding of new grasses was a slow project. The partial blocking of the harbour entrance had the good effect of creating a more protected harbour. However, it forced the building of a new sewerage scheme because the natural tidal clearance of the harbour was reduced.

The continuing reconstruction of Heimaey is interesting in illustrating a determined effort to save an island's economy from ruin by a volcano.

Tristan da Cunha

Tristan da Cunha is a small island in the South Atlantic. On 14 September 1961, earth tremors were reported, and on October 9th the ground was seen to be cracking. On the following day the volcano was visibly erupting, and the entire population of 260 was evacuated to Nightingale Island, 30 km away. On October 11th the islanders were forced to leave by ship for Cape Town and from there they were taken to England.

This volcano was thought to be extinct, but the eruption was sudden and violent. Lava spread over farming land and the crayfish canning factory, the island's only industry. Although the eruption did not take human life, it had a profound effect on the way of life of the people. This remote island was inhabited only by the descendants of a Corporal Glass who in 1817 remained on the island after a marooned military party was rescued from it. The 260 inhabitants mostly belonged to eight intermarried families.

The sudden upheaval of this small, independent, inward-looking society was said by some observers to be like throwing them from the nineteenth century into the middle of the twentieth century. The contrasts they found in Britain with their own quiet life on the island can be easily imagined: motor cars, huge cities, consumer goods, and thousands of unfamiliar faces. Although the British showed official and personal friendliness towards the islanders (including gifts, donations and an audience with the Queen) these did not compensate for their worries. Complications of jobs and money baffled the islanders.

As they left Britain to return to the island sixteen months after the eruption, their leader commented on English life — 'Money, money, money; worry, worry, worry, all the time'. The older islanders talked wistfully of the peace they had enjoyed in Tristan before the volcanic eruption drove them away.

It was the young people who showed the most evidence of being affected by their stay in Britain. Girls who had arrived wearing shapeless dresses and stockings of white wool returned with nylons, stiletto heels, handbags, transistor radios and record players. The administrator of the returning group commented that 'some islanders had spent money on rather unnecessary things'.

A few islanders, on reaching Tristan again and seeing their houses and gardens scattered with pieces of volcanic debris, and the fish-canning factory and beaches covered in lava, decided to return to Britain. Most, however, were pleased to return to their quieter, self-sufficient way of life. They took with them three tonnes of seed potatoes, ten tonnes of groceries and dozens of tools, and talked in a determined way of starting again.

■ DISCUSSION

1 What aspects of society in Britain would have been strange to the Tristan islanders?

2 What would be the daily life pattern of a Tristan islander or another isolated self-sufficient group of people?

3 What aspects of agriculture in a country such as Britain would have been strange to the islanders?

The love and tragedy of a volcano

Mayon

Volcanoes are not always seen solely as sources of destruction and catastrophe. The Mayon volcano in the Philippines provides a good example. Eruptions of Mayon were recorded in the following years: 1616, 1766, 1767, 1800, 1814, 1827, 1835, 1846, 1851, 1855, 1858, 1868, 1871, 1872, 1873, 1881, 1885, 1886, 1887, 1890, 1892, 1893, 1895, 1896, 1897, 1900, 1928, 1938, 1947, 1957 and 1968. In the last eruption balls of fire shot upwards and streams of lava flowed down the slopes, covering fields and crops.

But, to the people below, Mayon is the giver of life enriching soil. They recognize the fertility of the soil around the volcano and use it to grow coconuts, abaca (used for making fibre) and vegetables on the slopes of Mayon. It is said in the Philippines that the village-folk never fear the wrath of Mayon — instead, in between eruptions, they sing hymns and pray to God to spare them from the fury of the volcano.

Gunung Agung

The island of Bali, on the east coast of Java, is dominated by Gunung Agung, the volcano held sacred by the Balinese. Religion in Bali is a strange mixture of ancient Hinduism mixed with *animism* (the belief that natural objects have souls), and ancestor worship. Every village, and in some places, every house has its own temple which is sacred to the memory of ancestors. Towers in the temples represent sacred mountains. On the slopes of the most sacred mountain, Gunung Agung, is the most sacred temple, Besakih.

Gunung Agung, like Mayon and hundreds of other volcanoes, is seen as a symbol of life and death. Its fertile slopes are covered with hundreds of terraces of rice, which can be cropped two or even three times a year. Around the villages luxuriant vegetable and fruit gardens flourish. In Balinese religion the bodies of the dead are cremated and their ashes thrown into the crater of Gunung Agung or into the sea. Men of the highest caste particularly request that their ashes should be returned to the sacred mountain.

In 1963, the supposedly dormant volcano erupted sending lava flows, boiling mud and ash down the mountain slopes. Villages were burned and submerged and the vital rice-fields were covered with layers of ash and lava. Here, the Balinese villagers saw the sacred Gunung Agung as the death-bringer, an irate god who must be treated with respect and reverence.

Volcanic soils

One of the reasons for the high loss of life in volcanic eruptions is the high density of population on the slopes of a volcano. The soils are often productive enough to allow people to grow enough food on small areas of land. On the slopes of Merapi, near Jogjakarta in Indonesia, the farmers and villagers retreat at each eruption but between eruptions gradually extend their farming land up the slopes.

The volcanic soils are often very fertile when lava flows and tephra are chemically *basic* (alkaline). When the rocks are *acidic* the fertility is much lower. Productive volcanic soils may be derived from basalt, a basic *igneous* rock. On a well-drained slope the physical properties of these soils are good, but they can be poor on a poorly-drained lava plain.

Tephra material which is basic can produce fertile soils. The tephra, consisting of small pieces of rock material mixed with dust and ash, is very porous. Therefore *weathering* (the breaking down of rock material into smaller pieces) can proceed much faster than in the case of solid rocks. Water can penetrate through the porous layers and aid in the physical and chemical weathering. In some areas the depth of weathering action may be up to 100 metres.

■ ACTIVITY

1 Draw a sketch map of population density in South-East Asia and indicate the distribution of volcanoes in the area.
2 Locate the areas of volcanic soils which are also densely populated. What crops would be grown in these areas?

3 TSUNAMIS AND STORM SURGES

From: **THE HIGH TIDE
ON THE COAST OF
LINCOLNSHIRE (1571)**

Jean Ingelow

The old mayor climbed the belfry tower,
   The ringers ran by two, by three;
'Pull, if ye never pulled before;
   Good ringers, pull your best,' quoth he.
'Play uppe, play uppe, O Boston bells!
Ply all your changes, all your swells,
   Play uppe "The Brides of Enderby".'

I looked without, and lo! my sonne
   Came riding downe with might and main:
He raised a shout as he drew on,
   Till all the welkin rang again,
'Elizabeth! Elizabeth!'
(A sweeter woman ne'er drew breath
Than my sonne's wife, Elizabeth.)

'The olde sea wall (he cried) is downe,
The rising tide comes on apace,
And boats adrift in yonder towne
   Go sailing uppe the market-place.'
He shook as one that looks on death:
'God save you mother!' straight he saith;
'Where is my wife, Elizabeth?'

'Good sonne, where Lindis winds away,
   With her two bairns I marked her long;
And ere yon bells beganne to play
   Afar I heard her milking song.'
He looked across the grassy lea,
To right, to left, 'Ho Enderby!'
They rang 'The Brides of Enderby!'

With that he cried and beat his breast;
   For, lo! along the river's bed
A mighty eygre reared his crest,
   And uppe the Lindis raging sped.
It swept with thunderous noises loud;
Shaped like a curling snow-white cloud,
Or like a demon in a shroud.

And rearing Lindis backward pressed
   Shook all her trembling bankes amaine;
Then madly at the eygre's breast
   Flung uppe her weltering walls again.
Then bankes came downe with ruin
   and rout—
Then beaten foam flew round about—
Then all the mighty floods were out.

So farre, so fast the eygre drave,
   The heart had hardly time to beat,
Before a shallow seething wave
   Sobbed in the grasses at oure feet:
The feet had hardly time to flee
Before it brake against the knee,
And all the world was in the sea.

Upon the roofe we sate that night,
   The noise of bells went sweeping by:
I marked the lofty beacon light
   Stream from the church tower, red and
      high—
A lurid mark and dread to see;
And awesome bells they were to mee,
That in the dark rang 'Enderby'.

They rang the sailor lads to guide
   From roofe to roofe who fearless rowed;
And I—my sonne was at my side,
   And yet the ruddy beacon glowed:
And yet he moaned beneath his breath,
'O come in life, or come in death!
O lost! my love, Elizabeth.'

And didst thou visit him no more?
   Thou didst, thou didst, my daughter deare;
The waters laid thee at his doore,
   Ere yet the early dawn was clear.
Thy pretty bairns in fast embrace,
The lifted sun shone on thy face,
Downe drifted to thy dwelling-place.

That flow strewed wrecks about the grass,
   That ebbe swept out the flocks to sea;
A fatal ebbe and flow, alas!
   To manye more than myne and mee:
But each will mourn his own (she saith),
And sweeter woman ne'er drew breath
Than my sonne's wife, Elizabeth.

Tsunamis

The old name for a *tsunami* was a 'tidal wave', a bad name because it contained two major inaccuracies. Firstly, they have nothing to do with the tide, and secondly they are not just one wave but a series of waves.

A tsunami may be started by an earthquake, a volcano or an earth slide, either underwater or on the land. The shock waves of the disturbance are transmitted to the surface of the sea where they cause waves which differ in a number of ways from an ordinary swell or wind-generated waves. Tsunamis may have a wave length of 160 km or more (in contrast to a wave length of 100 to 300 metres for an ordinary sea-wave). They travel at speeds of up to 800 km/h, whereas ordinary waves travel up to only 100 km/h. In open ocean, tsunamis are almost undetectable because of their small amplitude in proportion

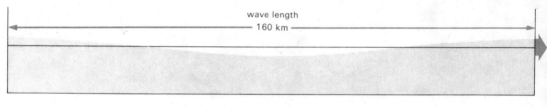

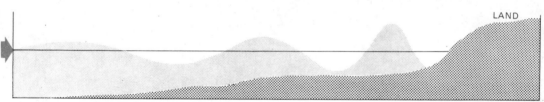

to their length. Thus, in Japan, in 1896, fishermen at sea noticed no unusual swell, but on returning to their villages found the coastal waters strewn with bodies of their families and wreckage of their houses.

The series of waves within a tsunami have been studied in some detail, particularly in the 1946 tsunami at Hilo, Hawaii. The time lapse between waves may be between fifteen minutes to an hour, and generally the first wave is only like a pronounced swell. Following this there is a sucking away of water from the shore as the first great trough arrives. The third to the eighth waves in the series are usually the largest.

People's belief that there is only one giant

Fig 3.1a) In open ocean a tsunami has enormous wave-length and almost undetectable amplitude. b) The amplitude increases dramatically as it nears land, producing a huge wave. The scale of diagram (a) is exaggerated.

wave has led to numerous deaths when people run to the shore while the great retreat of water in the trough is taking place.

A tsunami warning-system now operates in the central Pacific based in Honolulu, Hawaii. It recorded fifteen tsunamis between 1946 and 1954. The recording of sea movements at each of the stations can be used to map the path of the tsunami and estimate the rate of approach. Authorities then issue the warnings. Such a warning saved many lives in Honolulu in 1952 when an approaching tsunami was detected.

Fig 3.2 Man (arrowed) swamped by a tsunami in Hawaii. (Photo: Herald & Weekly Times Ltd)

Fig 3.3 Woodcut of a tsunami by the nineteenth century Japanese artist Hokusai.

Storm surges

The *storm surge* is a period of particularly high sea level and high waves which are sometimes misnamed 'tidal waves'. Unlike tsunamis they do not originate from movements of the earth's crust. Instead they originate just like any other sea-wave, being generated by wind. However they differ from ordinary sea-waves in three important ways:

● The waves are built up by strong winds. When the speed of the wind is very high, and the *fetch* (the distance of open sea it can blow across uninterrupted) is great, the waves increase greatly in size. In open ocean waves as high as 35 metres have been recorded.

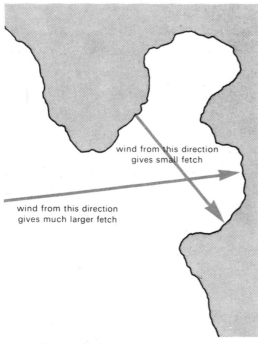

Fig 3.4 How *fetch* affects a storm surge.

● Atmospheric pressure can increase the size of the waves. A drop of 34 millibars in air pressure allows a rise of about 30 cm in the level of the sea. Because the winds of tropical cyclones and most mid-latitude storms are circulating around low-pressure cells, this is a characteristic which often accompanies high winds.

● Onshore winds piling up the sea against the coast are helped by confined areas (bays, gulfs, etc.) and shallowing bottoms.

This combination of factors tends to produce a storm surge, which may be anything from heavier-than-normal seas to a fifteen metre surge. Most tropical cyclones have a storm surge associated with them as they strike the coastline. As the example below shows, it was the surge which caused the greatest devastation in the Bay of Bengal in 1970.

If there is a large volume of water from rivers trying to flow into the sea, the storm surge may hold this back, causing flooding on coastal plains. A period of high tide may also coincide with a storm surge, adding to its intensity. Possibly the incident in "The High Tide on the Coast of Lincolnshire" was due to this.

ACTIVITY

Use a ripple tank to simulate normal waves and then the higher waves which could be characteristic of a storm surge. If rivers are also set up as shown below — what is the result?

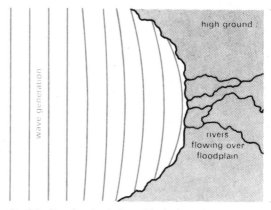

Fig 3.5 Plan for simulation with ripple tank.

Bay of Bengal

The people called it Black Thursday; that is, those who survived. The death-toll was one of the highest of any natural disaster — over 300 000.

The storm surge was caused by a tropical cyclone which moved northwards up the Bay of Bengal, its winds reaching 240 km/h, and building up before it a mass of water seven metres high. At the head of the bay is the Ganges Delta, made up of dozens of small low-lying islands, and the mouths of the many distributaries of the River Ganges.

Across the islands the waves surged, crushing and sweeping away people and their possessions. Then they poured across the low-lying alluvial flats of the Delta area, demolishing hundreds of villages.

In one compound of 36 people, 27 died in the surge of water. Survivors clung to bamboo trees as their flimsy houses were washed away. Some people saw the sudden flood as signifying the approach of doomsday, as they were surrounded by the floating bodies of men, women, children, cattle, oxen and chickens.

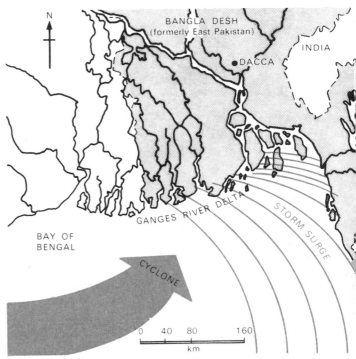

Fig 3.6 Storm surge in the Bay of Bengal, 1970.

Fig 3.7 The aftermath: survivors file past victim. (Photo: UPI)

The official statistics show that 9000 fishing boats were wrecked, 350 000 oxen and 150 000 cows were killed. Many ploughs, the basic tool of agriculture in the area, were swept away. Eighty per cent of the rice crop was ruined, and the land on which it was grown was badly affected. As well as the sea-wrack and debris which had been cast up onto the fields, salt had entered the soil. The land was useless for conventional agriculture until a long period of soaking rains had washed the salt through the soil.

What do national governments do in this kind of disaster? Pakistan's President, Yahya Khan, responded immediately by assigning the army to relief work. The military began dropping food and supplies from the air but much was smashed on impact. Roads had to be repaired or rebuilt before effective relief operations could begin.

An appeal to the United Nations brought aid from the rest of the world. Fifty countries sent

Fig 3.8 Devastation after Bay of Bengal storm surge. (Photo: Unicef)

help amounting to nearly $50 million. Australia sent emergency relief of $25 000, together with 5000 tonnes of wheat and 210 000 doses of cholera and typhoid vaccine. The U.S.A. sent immediate supplies of blankets, tents, wheat and cooking-oils. Later, when it was found that some low-saline areas of land could support vegetables, the U.S.A. provided seeds which could be used.

For the long-term relief of the area, to overcome the destruction of much of the economic base, the World Bank provided an interest-free loan of $22 million. With this it was hoped that the roads, fishing industry, communications and settlements could be rebuilt and repaired.

Fig 3.9 Large steamer tossed into field by storm surge. ▶ (Photo: UPI)

Erosion by the sea

Although coastal areas may occasionally be affected by a tsunami or storm surge, a more constant feature is erosion by waves. The sea has an influence on every coastline, both eroding and depositing material. The changes may take place over hundreds of years or within a few days.

It is convenient to divide coastlines into two main classes: those in the form of cliffs and those consisting of beaches. Coastal cliffs are an indication of a retreating coastline. The power of the waves acts at the base of the cliff and undermines it. The upper levels of the cliff are affected by spray and run-off from rainfall. The rate of retreat of cliffed coastlines depends on the resistance of the rocks and the power and duration of strong wave action.

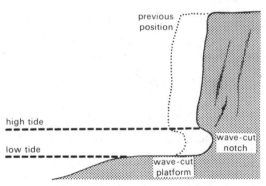

Fig 3.10 Erosion of cliffed coastline.

Coastlines consisting of beaches are those where *deposition* is most influential. Material eroded and transported by the sea is deposited as pebbles or sand. In some areas the beaches (zones of deposition) are only in small bays between cliffed headlands (e.g. the Sydney coastline). In other areas, long, continuous stretches of beaches have been built up (e.g. the Adelaide coastline).

The action of waves on beaches may vary over quite a short time-period. Some beaches in the U.S.A. and Southern Australia are stripped of most of their sand during winter storms but are built up again by quieter summer seas. The difference in action by constructional and destructional waves is shown in the diagram.

The sudden destructive action of heavy seas may be disastrous to areas where buildings are close to the waterfront. Sandy beaches often have several sand-dunes, inland from the beach, and parallel to it, which have been built up by wind action. These provide a reservoir of sand for the beach. However, in areas of intense urban or tourist development, the sand-dunes have been levelled and built on. In some areas, such as the Gold Coast of Queensland and the coastlines of most of Australia's capital cities, buildings front onto the beach. To protect these buildings from the sea, walls have sometimes been built. These, however, may not be sufficient to resist battering by the waves. There is documented evidence of waves hurling rocks of 3000 kg over a wall eight metres high at Cherbourg in France. At Wick, in Scotland, an 800 tonne block of concrete secured to a foundation was lifted and dumped into the harbour. The rebuilt breakwater was capped with a 2600 tonne mass, but this was removed by another storm.

The destructive power of the sea is usually greatest when there are strong on-shore winds, high tide and low atmospheric pressure — the storm surge conditions. It follows that in many coastal urban areas, the main danger of the storm surge may be erosion rather than inundation.

Fig 3.11 Waves erode (a) or build up (b) depending on the pattern of particle movement within the breaking wave.

4 TROPICAL CYCLONES AND TORNADOES

TYPHOON

Joseph Conrad

An extract from the novel

Through a jagged aperture in the dome of clouds the light of a few stars fell upon the black sea, rising and falling confusedly. Sometimes the head of a watery cone would topple on board and mingle with the rolling flurry of foam on the swamped deck; and the 'Nan-Shan' wallowed heavily at the bottom of a circular cistern of clouds. This ring of dense vapours, gyrating madly round the calm of the centre, encompassed the ship like a motionless and unbroken wall of an aspect inconceivably sinister. Within, the sea, as if agitated by an internal commotion, leaped in peaked mounds that jostled each other, slapping heavily against her sides; and a low moaning sound, the infinite plaint of the storm's fury, came from beyond the limits of the menacing calm. Captain MacWhirr remained silent, and Jukes's ready ear caught suddenly the faint, long-drawn roar of some immense wave rushing unseen under that thick blackness, which made the appalling boundary of his vision...

He watched her, battered and solitary, labouring heavily in a wild scene of mountainous black waters lit by the gleams of distant worlds. She moved slowly, breathing into the still core of the hurricane the excess of her strength in a white cloud of steam — and the deep-toned vibration of the escape was like the defiant trumpeting of a living creature of the sea impatient for the renewal of the contest. It ceased suddenly. The still air moaned. Above Jukes's head a few stars shone into a pit of black vapours. The inky edge of the cloud-disc frowned upon the ship under the patch of glittering sky...

'What's that? A puff of wind?' — it spoke much louder than Jukes had ever heard if before — 'On the bow. That's right. She may come out of it yet.'

The mutter of the winds drew near apace. In the forefront could be distinguished a drowsy waking plaint passing on, and far off the growth of a multiple clamour, marching and expanding. There was the throb as of many drums in it, a vicious rushing note, and like the chant of a tramping multitude.

Jukes could no longer see his captain distinctly. The darkness was absolutely piling itself upon the ship. At most he made out movements, a hint of elbows spread out, of a head thrown up.

Captain MacWhirr was trying to do up the top button of his oilskin coat with unwonted haste. The hurricane, with its power to madden the seas, to sink ships, to uproot trees, to overturn strong walls and dash the very birds of the air to the ground, had found this taciturn man in its path, and, doing its utmost, had managed to wring out a few words. Before the renewed wrath of winds swooped on his ship, Captain MacWhirr was moved to declare, in a tone of vexation, as it were: 'I wouldn't like to lose her.'

Fig 4.0 Hurricane over the Atlantic photographed by Skylab astronauts, September 1973. (Photo: NASA) ▶

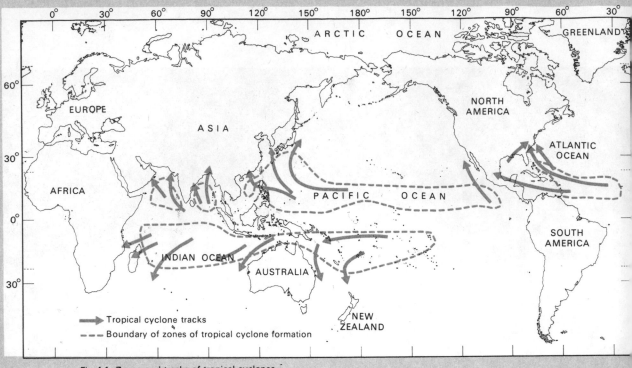

Fig 4.1 Zones and tracks of tropical cyclones.

Tropical cyclone tracks
Boundary of zones of tropical cyclone formation

Tropical cyclones

Tropical cyclones are called by a variety of names. In the U.S.A., Mexico and the Caribbean, they are called *hurricanes*; in the western North Pacific and China Sea areas they are called *typhoons*.

Fig 4.2 Basic pattern of air movement in a cyclone.

13 000 metres

13 000 metres

outflow

stream flow

rising air

eye

160 km   1 to 32 km   160 km

gales gradually decreasing

hurricane winds

gales gradually increasing

However, in the Australasian, Indian and African regions they are generally referred to as *tropical cyclones*.

Fig 4.2 shows a cross-section of a tropical cyclone. In the centre is the *eye*, the region of lowest pressure. The eye is calm and often has no cloud-cover. The width of the eye can vary from a few kilometres to more than 150 km in diameter but the average diameter is about 30 km.

Around the eye is a wall of cumulonimbus clouds where winds may exceed 300 km/h, accompanied by torrential rainfall. This zone extends about 80 km from the eye and causes destruction on a vast scale. Gale-force winds may be experienced up to 1000 km ahead of the path of the cyclone but they do not extend far behind the maximum-speed ring after a cyclone has passed.

Coriolis force

The circular formation of tropical cyclones and tornadoes is closely related to a phenomenon known as *coriolis force*. The rotation of the earth on its polar axis causes a deflection in winds and air currents. If the earth was not rotating, winds

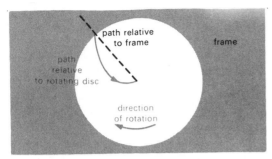

Fig 4.3 Disc demonstrating Coriolis Force.

would blow in a straight line from a high-pressure area to a low-pressure area, but the rotating movement of the earth causes this path to curve. A similar effect can be seen by moving a pencil in a straight line from the edge to the centre of a rotating disc or circular piece of cardboard. The pencil lines produced on the disc can be compared with the deflection of air currents as they move towards a low-pressure area.

If the disc is spinning in a clockwise direction, the deflection will be to the left; if rotation is anticlockwise, deflection is to the right. Similarly, in the Northern Hemisphere air currents are deflected to the right of the original line of motion, and in the Southern Hemisphere they are deflected

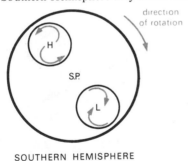

SOUTHERN HEMISPHERE

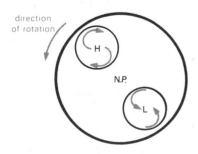

NORTHERN HEMISPHERE

Fig 4.4 Air circulation around high and low pressure systems.

to the left. Thus a low-pressure area attracting air currents from all sides will set up a clockwise rotating movement in the Southern Hemisphere and an anticlockwise movement in the Northern Hemisphere. The circular movement of air currents is clearly indicated by the cloud patterns in satellite photographs.

How tropical cyclones develop

Tropical cyclones occur in a relatively limited area. It has been found that the surface temperature of the sea must be greater than 25°C for a tropical cyclone to develop. This limits the area of origin to between the latitudes of 20°S and 20°N. But tropical cyclones never originate on the Equator or within about 8° latitude of it. Furthermore, they always develop over oceans, so the zone of cyclone development is limited to ocean regions between 8°S and 20°S, and between 8°N and 20°N.

Even then, tropical cyclones only develop in these regions under a very finely balanced set of atmospheric conditions. During summer in Australia the *thermal equator* moves southward. Where the south-easterly and north-westerly winds converge in this zone, many local *depressions* (low pressure cells) develop. A very few of these develop into tropical cyclones.

In any depression, air flows slowly in a spiral into the centre, forcing excess air to rise. For a tropical cyclone to develop from such a depression, the winds and pressure pattern at upper levels must remove air faster than it is flowing in. This causes lower air pressure on the surface of the sea. In turn the winds get stronger and the low pressure intensifies further until a powerful tropical cyclone has developed.

Tropical cyclones move generally westward, except in parts of the Indian Ocean (fig 4.1), at about 8 km/h. When they reach the coastline, they tend to change direction and slow down. The change from the sea surface to a land surface also rapidly weakens the tropical cyclone. Its wind speed slackens and the pressure in the eye rises. The tropical cyclone changes into a rain depression which may pour quantities of rain from the cumulonimbus clouds. By this stage the danger from gales has passed, but flooding of rivers can still be a problem. The rain depressions may settle in one place for a few days, or they may move slowly over a wide area, or they may disappear quickly.

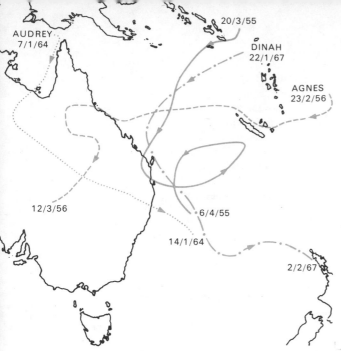

AUDREY
7/1/64

20/3/55

DINAH
22/1/67

AGNES
23/2/56

12/3/56

6/4/55

14/1/64

2/2/67

Fig 4.5 Cyclone tracks in the eastern Australian region.

Not all tropical cyclones move inland when they hit the coast. Sometimes they travel parallel to the coast for some time and then move out to sea again. The tracks in fig 4.6 show the variety of paths taken by tropical cyclones.

■ ACTIVITY

1 What is the 'thermal equator'? Why does it move? How does it limit the formation of tropical cyclones? (Reference books will be needed for this.)

2 Make a model of a tropical cyclone to scale. Use cotton wool and wire. If it is moved across a map of the same scale its widespread effects can be plotted.

3 Collect a set of weather maps from newspapers during the November-April period when a tropical cyclone is reported. Trace its path on the maps.

4 Simulate the coriolis force effect using a rotating disc and pencil.

Fig 4.6 Hurricane, Miami Beach, Florida. (Photo: American Red Cross)

Cyclone warning system

The Bureau of Meteorology in Australia has established a special Tropical Cyclone Warning System. Centres are located at Brisbane, Darwin and Perth. The information for the system comes from these sources:

1 Observations of weather conditions made at surface stations by observers.

2 Observations made by automatic weather stations. These are in remote localities such as the outer Barrier Reef. They report by radio every six hours.

3 Observations from Ships and Aircraft.

4 Observations by *radiosonde* balloons of the upper atmosphere.

5 Use of radar which can detect falling rain.

6 Photographs from meteorological satellites of cloud patterns.

7 Use of microseisms. These are very small earthquake-like tremors, produced by tropical cyclones, which can be recorded by especially sensitive seismographs.

When a tropical cyclone appears likely to develop a 'Tropical Advisory' is prepared and issued to shipping or the general public. A 'Flash Warning' is issued when a cyclone has definitely established itself within 800 km of the coast. This is the top priority warning broadcast by radio and television stations to the public, by coastal radio to shipping, and by aviation centres to all aircraft. Cyclone Warnings' are then issued every six hours at first and thereafter every three hours, until the danger has passed and a 'Final Warning' is issued.

Fig 4.7 Automatic weather stations like this one on Frederick Island, in the Great Barrier Reef, give advance warning of pressure changes which may herald a cyclone. (Photo: Australian Bureau of Meteorology)

'Ada'

Tropical cyclone 'Ada' hit the Whitsunday Islands tourist resorts on Saturday and Sunday the 17th and 18th of January, 1970. A very small but intense cyclone, it left in its path the ruins of houses, hotels, motels and the tourist industry of the Islands.

The progress of 'Ada' can be traced from the map (fig 4.9) and the following description.

Between Monday the 5th and Thursday the 15th of January a disturbance over the Coral Sea was tracked by satellite cloud photographs. At that time it was not possible to say accurately whether it was a tropical cyclone or a weak tropical depression.

On Thursday the 15th of January and Friday the 16th of January satellite observations gave some evidence that the disturbance was cyclonic activity. Warnings were issued to shipping.

By Saturday the 17th of January reports from the automatic weather station at Marion Reef (see fig 4.9) indicated a wind speed of 80 km/h. A public 'Flash Cyclone' warning was issued at 5 a.m. It was distributed to radio and television stations, police, fishing and harbour authorities, lightkeepers, postmasters and meteorological offices. These warnings were renewed every three hours.

At 11 p.m. Hayman Island reported winds of 95 to 115 km/h and by 1 a.m. the barometer had fallen to 976 millibars. In the Royal Hayman Hotel, guests were moved from the lounge to the dining-room just before the roof began to lift and plate glass windows smashed. It was estimated that soon after midnight the wind speed at Hayman Island increased to 160 km/h in gusts.

On Sunday the 18th of January, at 2.30 a.m., the cyclone was close to South Molle Island and lifted the roofs off tourist cabins. Because the island was in the path of the eye of the cyclone, it experienced two distinct blows with a period of calm in between. During the lull, people tried to find buildings which could resist the winds. Some sheltered for the night in the concrete toilet blocks which were the strongest structures on the island.

The next island hit was Daydream Island where again there was a brief period of calm between the two furious attacks of the cyclone.

Fig 4.8 Daydream Island after 'Ada'. (Photo: Brisbane Courier Mail)

The destruction is shown in fig 4.8. Not only were cabins demolished, but trees had leaves and branches stripped from them.

About 5 a.m. 'Ada' crossed the coast of the mainland tossing anchored vessels ashore and wrecking housing. Heavy rain fell as the cyclone passed through, and even heavier rain fell south of Bowen in the next two days. The heaviest 24-hour total recorded was 869 mm, a near-record figure for Australia. Roads and railways were put out of action by flooding, and power and water supplies were cut off.

Throughout the day the rain continued to fall, accompanied by winds of up to 90 km/h, while 'Ada' moved slowly towards the south. Late in the evening the cyclone showed signs of breaking up, but the rain was to continue for some time. The Bureau of Meteorology issued warnings until 4.15 p.m. on Monday. The final cyclone warning stated: 'Tropical cyclone "Ada" 29.7 inches (1006 millibars) was centred at 3 p.m. near Mirani about 20 miles north-west of Mackay and continuing to lose intensity. Wind gusts should decrease to below gale-force but heavy to flood rains continue along the lower Central Coast. Withdraw pennants'.

Tourism is a major industry of coastal Queensland and particularly the Whitsunday Island area.

destroyed. Even much further south, out of the cyclone's path, Lindeman Island and Brampton Island were battered by high winds and heavy seas. The gardens and the trees of the islands were stripped, and many groves of coconut palms on Hayman Island had disappeared.

The damage wrought by 'Ada' was estimated to be $12 million, and thirteen lives were lost. Some of the damage to the tourist industry was irreparable. Visitors were naturally reluctant to holiday in the area in the cyclone-prone months of January, February and March. The re-growth of the natural vegetation, too, was a slow process. However, the reconstruction of buildings was accomplished remarkably quickly. South Molle was operating again by Easter, Hayman Island by June and Daydream Island by August. But the scars of 'Ada' were still to be seen.

■ **ACTIVITY**

1 Trace the path of Ada on the map and calculate its speed throughout its journey. Draw a graph to show the variations in speed from the 15th of January to the 19th of January, using the six-hourly locations of the cyclone eye on the map.

2 'Ada' was dismissed in its early stages as only a small cyclone, a 'flea-bite'. Is it true that the size of a cyclone determines its destructiveness or intensity?

3 What other problems for the tourist industry in the Whitsunday Islands were created by 'Ada'?

Its resources are the beaches, warm climate, tropical islands, pleasant scenery and the man-made additions of hotels, cabins, yachts and pleasure cruisers, gardens and swimming pools.

After the January weekend of 'Ada', Hayman Island was left with most of its accommodation unroofed and badly damaged. Daydream Island had only the dining-room of the hotel useable, and South Molle had all its accommodation

Fig 4.9 The track of Cyclone 'Ada'.

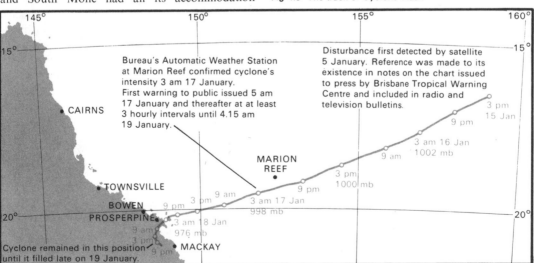

'Tracy'

In the early hours of the morning of Christmas Day 1974, Cyclone 'Tracy' hit the coast of Northern Australia, travelling almost directly over the city of Darwin. The winds of 200 km/h wrecked the city, causing one of the worst natural disasters in Australia's history. The death toll was about fifty and the houses of Darwin's suburbs were almost all destroyed. Most houses lost roofs, many lost walls and some disintegrated completely.

Warning of the cyclone was broadcast on Christmas Eve as 'Tracy' approached the coast of the Northern Territory. Darwin people listened to the warnings but were not unduly worried because recent cyclones had brought only moderately high winds and heavy rain. Only two weeks before, a cyclone had crossed the coast without causing any appreciable damage.

Cyclone 'Tracy' was different. During the late hours of Christmas Eve the winds steadily increased. By midnight the trees were being stripped of their leaves and branches, and torrential rain was blown

Fig 4.10 Darwin after 'Tracy'. (Photo: Advertiser News-papers Ltd)

almost horizontally into houses. Families gathered for protection in the smallest and strongest rooms of their houses, such as the bathroom.

At about 2.30 a.m. there was a lull as the eye of the cyclone passed over. Some people left their homes during the lull to look at the damage. Although the damage was extensive, houses were still standing. The calm of the eye ended at about 3.00 a.m., as the wind built up quickly from the opposite direction. Scattered pieces of roofing and other wreckage were picked up by the wind and smashed against houses.

The wind now became much stronger than in the first period of the cyclone, reaching a speed which wrecked the anemometer used to record wind velocity at the Bureau of Meteorology. Whole roofs were wrenched from houses and fibre-board walls were quick to follow. Cars were overturned

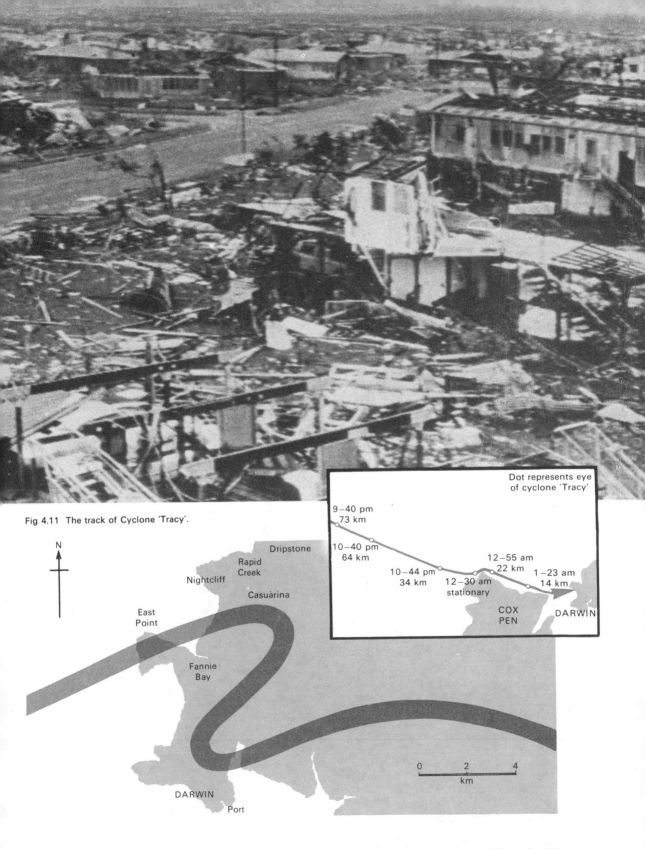

Fig 4.11 The track of Cyclone 'Tracy'.

N

Dot represents eye
of cyclone 'Tracy'

9–40 pm
73 km

10–40 pm
64 km

10–44 pm
34 km

12–30 am
stationary

12–55 am
22 km

1–23 am
14 km

COX
PEN

DARWIN

Dripstone

Rapid
Creek

Nightcliff

Casuárina

East
Point

Fannie
Bay

DARWIN

Port

0   2   4
km

as wreckage crashed into them. Many brick-walled buildings were also wrecked as they were battered by flying debris. All overhead power lines were brought down and telegraph poles were twisted and toppled. Fifty people died in the wreckage of their homes or on boats which were in Darwin harbour during the cyclone.

The rest of Australia gradually learned about Darwin's destruction during Christmas Day. Because normal communications were cut, the first news from Darwin came from the radios of ships in the harbour. It was not until 12.25 p.m. that the first official message came from Darwin authorities. The message read: 'Darwin completely devastated by cyclone last night. Deaths to date in neighbourhood of twenty. Ninety per cent of houses completely or seriously damaged. Suggest Natural Disaster team flown Darwin immediately'.

The 'team' referred to was the Natural Disasters Organisation which had been officially formed only nine weeks previously. It was under the command of Major-General A. B. Stretton and was set up to co-ordinate all emergency services immediately following a disaster. Major-General Stretton and a medical team flew to Darwin on the afternoon of Christmas Day, followed by other R.A.A.F. aircraft with medical supplies and communications equipment. These were the first of the many plane-loads of people bringing help to the city. Major-General Stretton took command of relief operations and was in charge of all parts of the city until December 31. With this post of command he could act swiftly to call for specific types of aid.

Because of the large proportion of houses wrecked, the first task was to find shelter for 30 000 of the city's population of 43 000. The schools, built mainly of brick, were largely undamaged and were quickly filled with homeless people. But the lack of sanitation and the threat of epidemics led Major-General Stretton to organise the evacuation of most of the homeless people from the city. The population of Darwin had to be reduced to about 15 000 or 20 000 — the largest number for whom shelter and facilities could be provided.

In the largest airlift operation ever attempted in Australia, 23 000 people were evacuated from the city in five days. Some left in their own cars, heading for Alice Springs or Adelaide, but most were flown out. The R.A.A.F. planes which brought in medical, sanitation and communications equipment returned to the southern cities filled with evacuees. Qantas, Ansett and T.A.A. aircraft also joined the operation, moving hundreds of people in each flight. The destination of the flights were determined by the needs of the people — evacuees were offered free flights to any capital city. When they arrived in Adelaide, Brisbane, Melbourne or Sydney, they were accommodated in hostels, camps and private houses.

Fig 4.12 Satellite view of 'Tracy'. (Photo: Advertiser Newspapers Ltd)

CYCLONE TRACY DIRECTLY ABOVE DARWIN

PERTH

BRISBANE

ADELAIDE

SYDNEY

MELBOURNE

The Darwin evacuees could bring few possessions with them; many had lost everything. However, they arrived in the southern cities to be met by voluntary organisations giving them clothes, food, toys, blankets and cash. Since news of the disaster reached the rest of Australia there had been a nation-wide response in the form of donations of money, goods, food and clothing. Some was sent directly to Darwin, but much was given to evacuees arriving by plane. The impact which the disaster had on the rest of the Australian population is well illustrated by the national television appeal held on New Year's Day which raised over $3 million in donations. Many other funds were initiated by other organisations, collecting hundreds of thousands of dollars.

The Federal Government was quick to recognise the plight of people moved to new cities without money, possessions or jobs. It offered a special payment of $31 weekly for all evacuees. People arriving at airports were handed cash to help them for the first few days.

Meanwhile, the remains of Darwin were being sprayed with disinfectant to prevent outbreaks of disease. Christmas food decaying in abandoned refrigerators and freezers was a source of concern. Dozens of police had been flown in from the other States to patrol the streets in order to discourage looting. The fleet of the Royal Australian Navy had sailed for Darwin and arrived on New Year's Day. The main task of the relief teams was to clean up the wreckage and debris and to collect and record any personal possessions or valuables.

One of the immediate questions was whether Darwin should be rebuilt on a new site. It was suggested that this was a good opportunity for a planned city, but there were strong arguments against this which finally swayed opinion in favour of rebuilding the old city. The buildings remaining in the city centre, the infrastructure (basic organisation) of public utilities and services, the private ownership of property and the tradition of the city all contributed to this decision.

The Government appointed a Darwin Reconstruction Commission, under the leadership of Sir Leslie Thiess, to plan the reconstruction of the city. One of the Commission's special tasks was to investigate the construction of housing best able to resist the effects of tropical cyclones. Feeling was very strong that when the next cyclone hit Darwin, the city would be much better prepared.

■ ACTIVITY

1 Collect reports on the rebuilding of Darwin. Discuss the problems which may arise in reconstructing the city.
2 Discuss the problems of looting, disease and evacuation in a disaster such as that caused by Cyclone 'Tracy'. How do you think these might be overcome?
3 Imagine yourself as an evacuee from Darwin. How would you react in such a situation?

Cyclone-proof buildings

The degree of devastation in Darwin was so great mainly because of the type of housing in the city and suburbs. Most of the houses were built of fibre-board, with corrugated iron roofing, and were raised on stilts. Sheets of roofing iron (or sometimes whole roofs) were ripped off and thrown against other houses. These and other loose objects, such as lawnmowers, became lethal missiles in the high wind, breaking open houses in their path. Once inside, the wind could wrench the entire house from its supports.

Brick and cement buildings, although damaged in the Darwin cyclone, were much more resistant to such battering. It was found, too, that buildings which had the roof securely bolted to the walls were even more resistant. At the James Cook University, research is being carried out in the Civil Engineering Department on cyclone-proof housing. The three most important requirements have been found to be:
●tying together the framework of the house
●securing the framework to the foundation
●ensuring that the roof is firmly bolted to the main structure
Various methods of achieving these requirements have been tried. 'Cyclone bolts' have been used to hold together the house frame. Plywood sheeting nailed to strategic points of the top and bottom beams of a house have been effective in a similar way. Other designers have advocated fibreglass modular units because, as continuous structures, they are resistant to high winds. The C.S.I.R.O. released a report on cyclone-proof housing in 1975, after several years of research.

Tornadoes...

Tornadoes are probably the most spectacular type of storm. They are certainly one of the most violent. Fortunately, however, they are restricted in their range. Although they occur in some form on all continents, it is the U.S.A. where they most frequently cause disaster.

It is possible to think of the tornado as a very intensified cyclone. It has an eye of very low pressure and a swirling belt of winds around it, but instead of spreading over hundreds of kilometres, the tornado's width may be only 2 km or less.

The very intense low pressure has often destroyed barometers, but a drop of 170 millibars has been recorded. The swirling winds of the tornado can only be measured with special electronic tornado-speedometers which have recorded winds of over 320 km/h.

The destruction by tornadoes is performed by the high winds, the strong updraught, and the low pressure, the last causing houses to explode as trapped air rushes out. Stories of the strange effects of tornadoes are many. They include observations of pieces of straw driven into wood, trains wrenched off the rails, an iron bridge lifted from its piers, animals lifted and carried 100 metres and chickens plucked of all their feathers. Many other reports can be found in newspaper reports or books on tornadoes.

What causes such an intense and localised phenomenon? It is generally thought that tornadoes form when two masses of different temperature and humidity meet. If the lower layers of the atmosphere are unstable, a strong upward movement of warmer air is formed. This starts to spiral as it rises, and the whole system intensifies. It seems that only a small percentage of these systems develop into the narrow, violent funnels of tornadoes. However, those that do develop into tornadoes travel in an irregular path over various distances. Some maintain their destructive power for many kilometres, others fade out quickly.

Fig 4.13 Tornado in Jasper, Minnesota. (Photo: courtesy Frank W. Lane) ▼

Fig 4.14 Narrow swathe of destruction cut by a tornado in Kansas. (Photo: AAP)

... in the U.S.A.

The midwest and southern regions of the United States experience periodic tornadoes which cause great local damage.

In April 1974, a cold frontal system triggered more than 100 tornadoes of varying sizes and strengths which caused the worst tornado disaster for fifty years. The death-toll was 331. The paths of the tornadoes can be traced from the map showing death tolls in each state (fig 4.15).

In Tennessee, the winds gained force in the valleys and gorges of the mountains and foothills, and caused more than forty deaths. In Alabama, the city of Jasper and the town of Guin were almost obliterated. The 'twisters' even extracted insulation from between the walls of houses and wrapped it around trees.

Five of the twelve States hit (Ohio, Alabama, Kentucky, Indiana and Tennessee) were declared major disaster areas under the scheme of national disaster relief which the United States Government instituted.

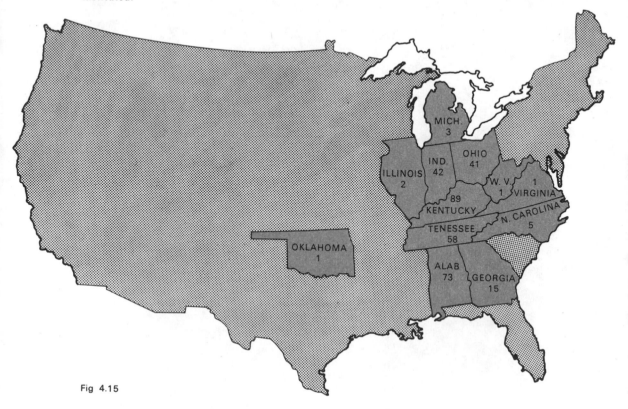

Fig 4.15

5 FLOOD

Run-off and floods

When rain falls, two things can happen to it on the surface of the earth. It can soak into the ground, or run across the surface. Seepage may be limited to the soil, but in areas of limestone and other permeable rocks, water can penetrate the bedrock. In such areas, there may be no surface run-off.

In most areas, however, there is a limit to the amount of water which can soak into the soil and underlying rock. Thus, whenever the quantity of rain (or melted snow) is greater than that which can be absorbed, a flood begins.

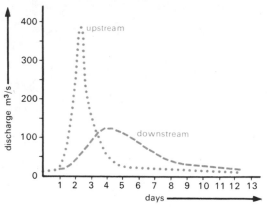

Fig 5.0 Variation in river height following heavy rain.

Two stages of a flood can be observed. The first *land phase* is the run-off of water across saturated soil. If it is in small channels it is called *rill-wash*; if it does not run in channels it is called *sheet-wash*. This stage occurs in the area of origin of the flood.

The *channel phase* of the flood follows closely when the surface run-off enters stream channels. These tributaries lead the floods into the main stream of the river. When talking of floods, people generally mean this phase. During the channel phase the inflow from the tributaries into the main river valley exceeds the outflow from the mouth of the river, and so the river level rises.

In upstream areas the flood wave is usually greatest in height but short in duration as it passes any one location. Downstream, the flood wave is dimished in height, but longer in duration.

Floods are a natural part of the water cycle and of the development of a river. In fact, we talk quite

often of 'flood plains', the large flat areas of alluvium deposited by the river near its mouth. Man has made use of flood plains in all parts of the world for agriculture. The fertility of the soil has often led to dense agricultural settlement on flood plains. The flatness of the flood plains, and the need to provide goods and services to the agriculturalists has led to the building of towns and cities on flood plains.

However, in the twentieth century people have sometimes forgotten that these are indeed *flood* plains, and have looked upon floods as something exceptional. Also, of course, buildings have been constructed up to the river banks. The river channel has been constricted with bridges, bridge piers, sewer outlets, pipelines and other obstructions.

Man has also altered run-off. The coating of large areas of soil with concrete, bitumen and buildings, as in the city, prevents natural seepage. Therefore provision for storm-water drainage through large underground channels has been made. This adds extra water to the river flowing through a city.

What is the solution to this continuing problem? If you read through the following accounts of floods, and study the photos, you may be able to assess the proposed plans for flood control.

■ ACTIVITY

1   Draw a sketch of a city or town area around a river that you know well, labelling all man-made features. (Include roads, bridges, buildings, lawns, footpaths.) Try to imagine what the area would have looked like before man settled the area. Draw a comparative sketch of the same view without its man-made features and with its original, natural vegetation.

2   Find an example of a flood plain in an atlas map. What uses has man made of it?

Fig 5.1 Cars swept down a Hong Kong street by a flash flood. Hong Kong floods are caused by very rapid run-off rather than the build-up in a whole river system. (Photo: Sydney Morning Herald)

The Nile

Floods are a natural part of the water cycle. This has been recognized for thousands of years. In Egypt the River Nile has been used for perhaps 5000 years as the source of life, and the annual flood has been the basis of this. As Shakespeare's Antony says:

> ...they take the flow o' th' Nile
> By certain scales i' th' pyramid; they know
> By th' height, the lowness, or the mean, if dearth
> Or foison follow. The higher Nilus swells,
> The more it promises. As it ebbs, the seedsman
> Upon the slime and ooze scatters his grain,
> And shortly comes to harvest.
> (*Antony and Cleopatra*, II. vii. 17–23)

Fig 5.2 shows the general pattern of the Nile's flood. The Blue Nile from the Ethiopian Mountains rises in response to heavy mid-year rains, and causes flooding in the Nile Valley. From July to October, floods occur along the Nile through the Sudan and Egypt.

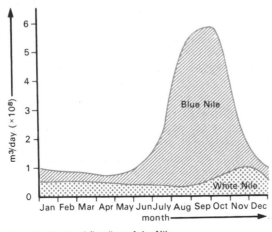

Fig 5.2 Seasonal flooding of the Nile.

The farmers along the Nile made use of the floods. Although the height and actual timing of the flood peak was not constant, there was a pattern which they could act upon. Houses were not built on the river banks. Instead they were placed 500 metres or more from the normal edge of the river, high enough and far enough to escape most of the floods. Here the houses did not take up valuable space which could be used for agriculture.

The agricultural land near the river was divided into fields separated by earth banks. When the Nile flooded, the water spread over the fields and as it retreated it was trapped in the small *basins* created by the banks. These were reinforced to keep in the water and small ditches were dug to carry water further from the river. In this way the water was allowed to seep gradually into the soil providing the basis of agriculture. At times of low-water, primitive lifting apparatus was used to raise water to the fields of growing crops.

Not only did the annual flood provide water for agriculture, but it also deposited a new layer of silt each year. In particular this occurred in the lower reaches of the river and the delta, and of course was what had originally built the delta. The additional layer of alluvium each year added to the ability of the soil to grow the quantities of food needed for the dense population of the Nile Valley.

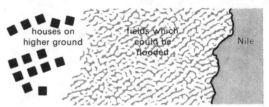

Fig 5.3 Settlement pattern on the Nile flood plain.

In some areas of the Nile Valley, this form of *basin agriculture* using flooding is still practised, but the building of the Aswan High Dam has changed things. The Dam was built to even out the flow of the Nile. Together with the use of power-driven pumps, it was intended to expand the agricultural land along the Nile.

■ DISCUSSION

1 Find out details on the building of the Aswan High Dam — the reasons for construction and the difficulties.
2 How would the people of the Nile Valley regard the flooding? Imagine yourself in their place.
3 What methods and machines did the Egyptians use for raising water from the river to basins in dry seasons?

Brisbane

Tropical cyclone 'Wanda' battered the Queensland coast in late January 1974. The people of the area were accustomed to at least two or three tropical cyclones during the summer season, but Wanda turned out to be different. The high winds of the cyclone were not the major danger this time. Instead it was the continual rain which poured from the massive cumulonimbus clouds onto already saturated river basins.

The cyclone hit the coast and moved southwards, as is the usual pattern, pouring tonnes of water onto coastal towns from Townsville to Brunswick Heads. However the cyclone and associated low-pressure systems also poured rain onto the western side of the Dividing Ranges causing flooding of the inland rivers through Queensland and N.S.W.

The usual pattern of tropical cyclones is that they break up after following the coast. Often, in Australia, they develop into a rain low-pressure

Fig 5.4 Brisbane suburb, January 1974. (Photo: Brisbane Courier Mail)

system which travels inland, gradually abating. Cyclone Wanda became a rain depression, but continued to pour rain on the mountains and coast near Brisbane. The catchment areas of the Brisbane River and its tributaries received a record rainfall. Brisbane itself received 635 mm in four days.

The newspaper clippings on pages 64 and 65 tell the story of the floods.

■ ACTIVITY

1 Using the newspaper clippings as a reference, tell the story of the floods in your own words.
2 Collect newspaper clippings for any natural disaster which has occurred recently. Display them in a similar way.

Late night crossing by cyclone

CYCLONE Wanda crossed the south Queensland coast north of Double Island Point last night, but there were no reports of damage.

At 9 p.m., Brisbane Weather Bureau said the cyclone was centred 40 kilometres (25 miles) north - east of Gympie.

Wanda, spotted by the Brisbane Weather Bureau late on Wednesday night, was moving southwest at 20 kilometres an hour (12 m.p.h.).

The bureau forecasters said the centre would continue moving southwest, and gradually weaken.

Gales of 60 to 65 kilometres an hour (40 to 45 m.p.h.) were expected to affect coastal areas between Double Island Point and Coolangatta until 9 a.m. today.

Heavy to flood rains were expected overnight along the coast from Gympie south, but were expected to ease early today.

The lighthouse keeper at Double Island Point told Tin Can Bay police last night that he estimated winds at more than 65 kilometres an hour (45 m.p.h.).

Brisbane Weather Bureau recorded 34 milimetres (133 pt.) between 9 a.m. and 9 p.m.

To clear

The bureau expects the cyclone's influence to clear from the metropolitan region today.

Forecasters said more settled weather should return to southern coastal areas by tomorrow.

Extracts from The Brisbane Courier Mail, January 1974.

FIG ARE

BRISBANE'S overworke night as State Gove beleaguered city's flood

The Brisbane River has since the flood emergency b more than six metres (21ft.

Brisbane-city of island suburbs

BRISBANE was a city of island suburbs last night, in the wake of the city's worst flooding.

Rain from cyclone Wanda dumped falls of more than 300 mm (12in.) on the city and suburbs in 12 hours yesterday — and rain continued last night.

Between 9 a.m. and 9 p.m., the Weather Bureau in Ann Street had recorded 168 mm (672 points).

Brisbane Weather Bureau director (Mr. A. J. Shields) said the floods had been the most disruptive in memory.

"The rain was so heavy over such a wide area, that flooding occurred in almost every watercourse," he said.

"The flooding was far more severe than in the June, 1967, or February and April 1972 floods."

The high tide at 10.37 a.m., swollen to king tide proportions by an 45 cm (18in.) surge from Moreton Bay, added to flood problems.

Showers tip

Brisbane Weather Bureau forecasters said that after more overnight rain, the rain depression left by cyclone Wanda — which ended north-west of Dalby about noon yesterday — should clear to showers today.

Every suburb in Brisbane had some area affected by the floods.

Water police used small boats with outboard motors, and civilian volunteers used dinghies to evacuate people from flooded homes in at least six suburbs.

In Windsor, homes were evacuated in Northey, Cullen and Thistle Streets and Swan Road; at Kedron from Swan Street; at Hawthorne Road, Hawthorne; and in areas of Sandgate and Brighton.

At Cribb Island, roofs were blown off, and far across the city at The Gap, householders dug trenches to stop floodwater entering the rear of homes in Bellata Street.

Roofs off

Homes at Redcliffe, Nundah and Wynnum lost roofing.

The city's business life came almost to a standstill, with absenteeism high — and the city's rain - lashed streets almost bare of people or traffic.

Drama day

Telephone delays were frequent, as thousands of people restricted to their homes tried to conduct business by phone.

In a day of drama:

Hundreds of residents of Windsor were evacuated as 4.5 (15ft. floods

surged through the suburb.

Breakfast Creek, Enoggera Creek, Kedron Brook, and Schultz's Canal set flood record levels.

Traffic came to a virtual standstill at dusk on the northern side of the city, with major roads, Bowen Bridge Road, Sandgate Road, and Abbotsford Road, closed by floods.

An emergency operations centre was set up at police headquarters to direct relief for flood victims.

Postmen in many suburbs could not reach homes to deliver mail — or did not attempt runs at all because of the bad conditions.

Most of the city's bus services were abandoned during the flooding peak because roads were impassable on most routes.

Electricity blackouts occurred at Kangaroo Point, Sandgate, and Macgregor when winds tore down power lines.

The R.A.C.Q. at noon appealed to motorists to keep off the roads until flooding eased.

Highest since 1955

The Brisbane River yesterday reached its highest peak since 1955.

At noon, the Harbours and Marine Department port office gauge, near the Bontanic Gardens, registered almost 3½ metres (10ft. 8in.).

This is about .9 metres (2ft. 8in.) above a high king tide level.

In 1955, the river height was 3.6 metres (11ft. 6in.) at the port office.

The tremendous volume of flood water rushing downstream caused havoc.

River users said they could not remember such savage turbulence.

...TERS
...EARY

...ency services were faltering last ... authorities warned that the ...uld last for several more days.

...ng continually in the upper reaches ... days ago and it is expected to rise to ...e Port Office about noon today.

This compares with a maximum of nine metres (29ft.) in the 1893 flood.

The Brisbane Weather Bureau last night predicted more rain — on top of the 639 mm (25.36in.) that had fallen from 9 a.m. on Wednesday until 8 p.m. yesterday.

Most State and private primary and secondary schools will not open until February 4 — a week late.

University supplementary examinations have been put back a week to Feb. 5.

The floods have crippled the city, leaving thousands of residents homeless, suburbs isolated, and essential services disrupted.

Hundreds of exhausted emergency personnel — including police, the military and volunteers — worked throughout yesterday combatting the floods which have affected one-third of the city and claimed four lives.

The plight of the city grew worse yesterday as one of its power stations, Tennyson, was shut down when floodwater swamped its main basement.

At least 17 suburbs have been blacked out by electricity supply failures.

Gas threat

Brisbane's gas supplies have been reduced to thousands of homes mainly in flood areas.

Thirty soldiers were sent to the Newstead gasworks last night when floodwaters threatened to cut the whole city's supply. The soldiers packed sand bags throughout the night.

Some areas of the city were also without reticulated water.

Brisbane's telephone services have been over-taxed during the crisis and thousands of subscribers are without telephone communication.

The raging flood tore several ships from their moorings in the Brisbane River.

The port has been closed by the flood and port authorities said that ships in the river may be trapped there for weeks because of massive silting at the river mouth.

Government authorities have been unable to estimate the full extent of the disastrous flooding but conservative estimates put the total homeless in Brisbane at about 4000.

City almost at standstill

THE Brisbane River's massive floodwave early today began its surge through the city's aleady-ravaged areas and authorities warned that the disaster level would not fall until late this afternoon.

Rescue craft last night were operating by searchlight to move scores of people trapped in flooded suburbs as the river height reached 6.7 metres (22ft.) — 4.2 metres (14ft.) above normal.

The rescue operations followed another day of heightening crisis in many suburbs as police and volunteers evacuated 600 more flood victims from their homes.

The worst floods this century claimed more lives bringing the State death toll to eight dead and two missing.

The raging Brisbane River continued to rip the heart out of the near-crippled city, tearing vessels from their moorings and washing into more than a dozen suburbs causing disruption to essential services.

FOOD RUSH

BRISBANE now faces a food shortage, as more than 5000 flood victims start to move back into their homes.

But the homeless were warned last night: "Don't go back to quickly."

Faced with possible danger from floodwaters until the week-end, the homeless may have to spend a total of eight days at crowded welfare centres.

The city's attempt to get back to normal after the disastrous holiday week-end flooding, ended in chaos as thousands of cars jammed main arterial routes and housewives went on shopping sprees.

The city is facing a shortage of bread and meat and fresh vegetables during the next few days. Milk already is being rationed on a rotation basis.

Only one of the city's three flour mills is operating and flour supplies to major bakeries are expected to be less than half the normal volume.

Slaughtering would continue today and tomorrow and there would be ample supplies for butcher shops.

It was not certain if supplies would be maintained after the week-end, he said.

A shortage was possible through panic buying and the difficulty in transporting stock to the city.

Supermarkets throughout the city were packed yesterday as housewives went on an unprecedented spree of panic buying.

Several stores were forced to close their doors to re-stock their shelves and there were reports of women buying several trolley loads of foodstuffs.

Earlier both the Premier and the Opposition Leader (Mr. Houston) had called on the public "not to over-react" and not to buy heavily, following reports of shortages of a number of foods.

$10 fine

POLICE yesterday began issuing $10 on-the-spot fines.

The tickets were for failing to obey a lawful direction.

A police spokesman said that a more serious example of the same offence could lead to a court appearance and a higher fine.

The Police Minister (Mr. Hodges) said complaints had been received from Army, civil defence and police.

Mr. Hodges said sightseers were parking their cars in areas restricting operations, damaging access roads and in some cases getting into trouble themselves.

River Murray

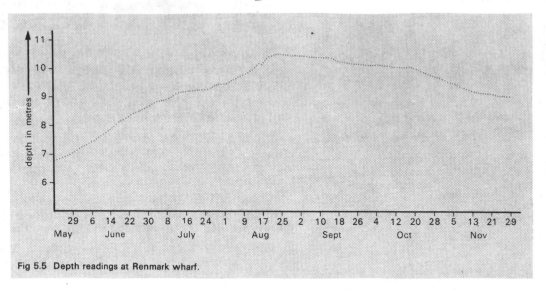

Fig 5.5 Depth readings at Renmark wharf.

Fig 5.6

The River Murray floods of 1956 were typical of river valley flood patterns, spreading outward from the river channel, breaching banks and levees fig 5.6), inundating low-lying areas (fig 5.7) and submerging the natural banks (fig 5.8). Sandbank levees (fig 5.9) contained the river at some points, but where floodwaters broke through, damage was considerable (figs 5.10 and 5.11).

Fig 5.7

Fig 5.11

Fig 5.10

Fig 5.9

Fig 5.8

Florence

There are many floods in the world each year on a similar scale to the Florence flood in 1966, but to people with knowledge of Florence's art treasures, this one was different.

In the catchment area of the River Arno, and its tributary the Sieve, rainfall equivalent to that of a normal four months fell on the days of November 2nd and 3rd 1966. Both of the rivers surged downward. On the upper Arno were two dams which were intended to regulate the flood. However, because the Penna Dam, upstream, opened its gates too late, it released more water than the Levane Dam could handle, so that its gates were thrown open also. This contributed to the sudden great rush of water which struck Florence early on November 4th.

As the river rose suddenly in the city, water spread through the streets, pouring into cellars and then through doorways and windows of houses. The surging force of the water broke open the bolted, heavy wooden doors of the Church of Ognissanti and began to batter the bridges, including the Ponte Vecchio, with oil-drums, trees and other debris.

The river had also flushed from flooded basements the thick black fuel-oil of central heating systems, mixing it with sewage. From upstream had come a great deal of sediment, and the carcasses of drowned animals, resulting in a slimy evil-smelling mixture which penetrated into houses, churches and galleries.

It flooded the Biblioteca Nazionale Centrale, Italy's largest library, engulfing one and a half million volumes. In the Museo di Storia della Scienza (Museum of the History of Science) the flood engulfed one of Edison's first phonographs, and original instruments of chemistry, medicine and physics. Many treasures were rescued, including Galileo's telescopes. In the Church of Santa Croce, Cimabue's thirteenth century painting 'Crucifix' was battered and destroyed, and other art treasures were streaked with oil stains. The altars before the tombs of Michelangelo and Galileo in Santa Croce were surrounded by the dark slime.

In the Uffizi, one of the world's greatest art

Fig 5.12 Extent of the disastrous flood in Florence, 1966.

galleries, the director and others tried to rescue 100 paintings from the restoration rooms, and to move a collection of self-portraits by Raphael, Titian, Rubens and others from the gallery nearest the Ponte Vecchio. It seemed that the Ponte Vecchio, the 600 year-old bridge lined with jewellery shops, would be swept away, taking part of the Uffizi gallery with it. Fortunately, despite heavy battering, the bridge remained.

The list of damage by the flood is long. It includes the submergence of millions of books, many of them invaluable single copies; the loosening of panels of the 'Doors of Paradise' on the Baptistery; the oil-staining of innumerable paintings, frescoes and sculptures; and the destruction of invaluable musical instruments and Etruscan artifacts.

The floodwaters ravaged the city for only one day. The reconstruction took months and years, involving firstly the clearing of mud and the retrieval of objects swept away, and then the expert work of restoration of books and artworks.

There was a rush of helpers and money from overseas. University students from all over Europe and experts from other museums went to Florence to help in the cleaning-up and restoration. $1.5 million was raised from world-wide donations. This aided the setting up of buildings with humidity and temperature control for art restoration. Here, oil stains, watermarks and mould were removed from paintings. Books were slowly dried and the pages separated and cleaned. Sculptures were cleaned, repaired and remounted on their bases.

The people of Florence who were most harmed by the flood were the small craftsmen who lived near the river. Their ancestors had settled there so that the river could power their small machines. With the aid of relief money, they returned to their original shops, setting up business again within a few weeks.

The reconstruction of the city, and in particular the restoration of artworks has been called 'The Miracle of Florence'. Technology, money and expertise were combined in a unique rescue operation.

■ ACTIVITY
1 Find reproductions of some of the famous artworks referred to above.
2 Discuss whether the large sum of money spent on restoration was justified.

Flood control

In the United States and the United Kingdom much research has gone into the prevention of disastrous loss of life and property by flood. This has resulted in the formation of river-valley authorities. Their task is to co-ordinate the use of a river system and to use the research of other groups of scientists to provide the residents of a valley with detailed information.

Professor Munro, the Honorary Director of the Water Research Foundation of Australia has listed a number of ways in which the effects of floods can be lessened:

● *Forecasting* — More stations collecting meteorological data can be set up on catchments to report regularly on the amount of water flowing into rivers.

● *Levee Systems* — This is the most widely used method (e.g. the River Nile levees) and is reliable if the levees are maintained. It is now relatively cheap, due to the efficiency of modern earth-moving equipment.

Fig 5.13 Flood watch: engineers monitor tide gauges on the River Thames to predict possible flood areas.

●*Large dams on large rivers* — These can be very effective in favourable topographical conditions, but are expensive.

●*Small dams on urban creeks* — These can prevent many medium sized floods, and are a good economic proposition.

●*River channel improvement and straightening* — This can reduce floods only in certain areas. It allows water to run through the improved channel more quickly but increases flood levels downstream.

●*Drainage works* — This is used where the main problem is water remaining on agricultural land for weeks after the flood has subsided.

●*Floodways* — These are man-made channels used to divert the overflow from rivers away from areas where it may cause harm.

●*Soil conservation and small dams on upper catchments* — This has limited value in floods caused by widespread rainfall.

●*Flood proofing buildings* — Houses on stilts are common in many areas. Other methods of preventing water from entering buildings are sometimes used in low-lying areas.

●*Zoning of flood plains* — Where there is plenty of flood-free land, building should only be carried out on higher land. Flood-prone land could be used for parks and playing fields.

■ DISCUSSION

Make a list of advantages and disadvantages of each of these schemes and compare them.

Fig 5.14 Floods undermine railway installations in the U.S.A., 1955. (Photo: American Red Cross)

Flood simulation

The map shows the city of 'Waterlog', which is troubled by periodic flooding, as shown. You are a city councillor. Three proposals have been put to Council.

● To encourage the people living in the 'regularly flooded' area to move to higher ground, marked A.

● To build a dam across the gorge to the west of the city, marked B on the map.

● To build a dam at C on the map, and a spillway at D, 45 m above sea-level.

■ ACTIVITY

1 The heights of the two dams are evident from the map. What are they?

2 Which proposal would provide the most complete answer?

3 Which proposal would have the greatest beneficial side-effects?

4 On the evidence before you, which scheme do you think the best?

5 What other questions would you have to ask before being sure you had chosen well?

6 What evidence might make you change the choice you made in question 4?

7 You are a millionaire industrialist. Where would you buy land a) for a new factory? b) for a new home?

8 You have a house on the river at E. Does this influence your decision?

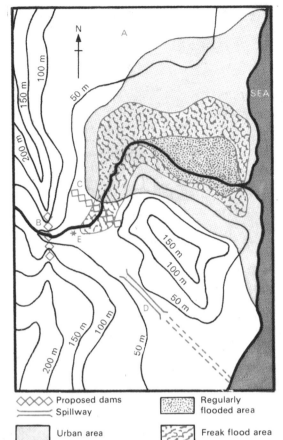

Proposed dams
Spillway
Urban area
Regularly flooded area
Freak flood area

Fig 5.15 Contour map of 'Waterlog'.

How large a flood can we afford to prepare for?

We can rarely, if ever, provide protection against the maximum possible floods, but these may occur only once every 10 000 years.

However a 'medium' flood occurring about every ten years can be prepared for without exorbitant cost.

Consider the economic terms in which planners see the question:

Fact I A major flood — once every 100 years — might cause $5 million damage within a river basin.

Fact II A medium flood — once every 10 years — might cause $1 million damage.

■ DISCUSSION

What is the average damage per year of these two types of flood? Why do Government agencies see it as good sense to protect against a medium flood, but an uneconomic proposition to provide for a major flood?

Floods and alluvial soils

Rivers are agents of *erosion*, *transportation* and *deposition* of rock material. Throughout much of the length of a river, rock material is continually being broken and picked up by the river. Some of it is carried only a short distance, but some material remains a part of the river's *load* until it reaches the flood plain near the river mouth.

In a flood, the volume of water and the speed of the river are both increased. The greater volume of water means that a greater *capacity* of material can be carried by the river. The higher speed allows larger particles to be transported (the *competence* of the river increases).

The speed of any river varies greatly from point to point along its course, but there is an overall increase from the head to the mouth. However, many of the largest pieces of rock are carried only short distances. The material which is carried out of mountain regions by the river is mostly clay, silt, sand and small gravel. The larger pieces of gravel and sand will be the first material deposited at any fall in speed of the river. Even in a flooded river, large rocks are quickly deposited on the river-bed. The finer silt and clay, however, may be carried out onto the surrounding plains by the flooding river and deposited there as the waters slow down. Thus the flood plains surrounding a river gain the deposits of the finest material during a flood.

This alone is not enough to make the soils fertile. The river also carries a large amount of organic material — small particles of plant and animal remains — and this is also deposited with the fine silt on the flood plain. The organic material provides a life-support for small organisms which in turn are consumed by larger organisms. The remains and waste-products of all these organisms add *humus* (decayed organic material) to the soil. Crops or pastures planted by man flourish in the highly fertile soil.

Two main problems are often present for those who farm the alluvial flood plains. Although they are fertile, the alluvial soils are only highly productive if they are well-drained. Because the height of the flood plain is very little above (in some cases below) the height of the river, this may be difficult. The other problem is that flood plains are still susceptible to floods, whether unused or farmed or built-on. The attraction of very productive soil has been the cause of great loss of life from flood in the densely-populated flood plains of China.

■ ACTIVITY

1   Research more information on rivers and draw a labelled diagram showing the parts of the river mentioned in the discussion above.

2   Find out more about the major Chinese rivers and the intensive agriculture on their flood plains.

3   Give examples of organisms which might live in the soil, or live on those in the soil.

4   What are levees? How are they formed? Why does man build them along some rivers?

Fig 5.16 Intensive rice farming in alluvial soil, Indonesia. (Photo: author)

6 DROUGHT

Fig 6.0 (Photo: Tony Hall, OXFAM)

What is drought?

Probably everyone knows that a drought involves a lack of rainfall, but let us see if we can define it more precisely.

Firstly, it should be established that we do not talk about a drought affecting a desert because we assume that a desert is in a state of perpetual drought. The areas which can be said to have a drought are those which have an average rainfall high enough to support agriculture or pastoralism. It is the irregular variation in the rainfall pattern which produces droughts.

In the United Kingdom, drought is described as any period having 15 consecutive days without rain, and in parts of the U.S.A., drought is a period of 21 days with 30 per cent or less of the average rainfall. However, in Australia the period of lack of rain may be months or years, and in fact there is almost always some part of Australia which is experiencing a drought.

A better definition of drought takes into account not only the lack of rainfall but also the high evaporation rate which may make rainfall ineffective. The potential evaporation (the amount of water which could be evaporated if it were there) in many parts of Australia far exceeds the average annual rainfall. A small decrease in rainfall in such a place could lead to drought conditions. Sometimes the amount of rainfall required to maintain enough soil moisture for particular plants has been used to define drought. This is a realistic definition, but difficult to apply in some cases.

■ ACTIVITY

Draw a graph to show the three sets of rainfall statistics shown below, using the same axes. Use different colour bars to distinguish the years.

Hawker, South Australia — rainfall in mm

Month	Average	1972	1973
January	20	120	16
February	28	11	131
March	16	0	39
April	20	1	22
May	26	7	47
June	32	12	71
July	31	27	71
August	29	45	81
September	20	6	38
October	23	12	69
November	24	2	16
December	14	4	23
Total	283	247	624

1 When is the low rainfall season for 1972 and 1973?

2 When is the low rainfall season for average years?

3 Comment on the variation from year to year and from the average.

4 Are the average figures useful for predicting monthly rainfall patterns?

5 Could the February to May period of 1972 be called a drought?

6 What other information besides rainfall statistics is needed before we can identify a drought?

Australia, 1964-66

The 1964–66 drought in N.S.W. and Queensland was one of the worst in recent times. However, the point is made elsewhere that drought is always present somewhere in Australia.

An appreciation of the devastation of the 1964–66 drought can be gained from the following facts:

● The cost of the drought to Australia was estimated to total $1,500 million
● Sheep numbers in N.S.W. were reduced by 16% and in Queensland by 22%
● The wheat yield in N.S.W. fell by 30% in one year
● Australia's wool cheque for 1965–6 fell by $27 million
● It was estimated that drought cost urban dwellers $1 million in food price increases

In addition to these there are other less obvious effects in any drought, but particularly in this one.

The death of cattle or sheep involves not only the loss of their monetary value, but also the loss of their breeding ability. This in turn may influence the general herd quality. The loss of expensive sown pastures can be another major disaster for pastoralists. Erosion by wind and later by water (when there is little stabilizing vegetation), can remove valuable topsoil from thousands of hectares of land.

■ ACTIVITY

1 Collect newspaper clippings on any droughts presently occurring.
2 Discuss the reasons why a drought in rural areas has an influence upon cities and urban-dwellers.

Fig 6.1 Receding water level in the Burrinjuck Dam, N.S.W. (Photo: Bureau of Meteorology)

BUSH DROUGHT, AUSTRALIA

Clive Sansom

Beyond the broad white rim of pond
And the frogs' croaking,
No water comes to the parched land
Though her lips are cracking.

An inch of sand to a fathom of rock
Is the earth's measure—
Dry white sand where the roots clutch
With a drowned hand's seizure.

Coarse grass and brush and stunted gum
Strive here for living.
No illusion of peace has Nature left,
No mask of loving:

Her face is harsh, dried hard and lined
By the drenching sun;
Beneath her pallid skin of dust
No smile is seen.

No shivering water adds its groove
To the rough sand-marking:
Only the dark and sudden stream
Of a blacksnake's making.

No sound of rainfall on dead leaves:
Only the arid notes
Of birds, and the bored frogs clacking
Their castanets.

Acknowledgement: Clive Sansom and Methuen & Co Ltd for 'Bush Drought, Australia', from *Witnesses and Other Poems*.

Overcoming the effects of drought in Australia

There has been a great deal of study of the drought problem in Australia and all kinds of possible solutions have been put forward. Here is a selection of them. Some have been proposed by official investigating bodies, others have come from off-the-cuff opinions by farmers and city-dwellers. Think about and discuss the possibilities and effectiveness of each one.

■ OPINIONS

1 Do not allow farmers and graziers to settle in areas where there is a likelihood of drought. Encourage them to use the coastal lands more intensively.

2 Establish a National Drought Research Institute which could be responsible for research into all aspects of drought and for supervising the implementation of the results.

3 Teach the study of weather as a major part of school courses in Australia. Emphasise the direct and indirect effects of drought, erosion and floods on everyone in the nation.

4 Set up solar energy sources near any water sources (periodic salt lakes or underground water) to allow the desalination of drinkable water supplies.

5 Place controls on the use of artesian water supplies by pastoralists, particularly in dry years.

6 Pour a large amount of money into primary industry in Australia to allow the development of equipment and techniques on the farm to resist drought.

7 Establish a national drought fodder reserve for supply to stock in dry years.

8 Undertake extensive cloud-seeding over drought areas to produce man-induced rain.

9 Preserve the natural drought-resistant plants and encourage the spread of those suitable for grazing. These may provide food for stock at times when introduced grasses would die from lack of water.

10 Introduce kangaroo-grazing to replace sheep because the kangaroo is much better able to cope with dry conditions.

These schemes are not necessarily to be recommended. Some are generally thought to be quite impossible and useless, while others have a great deal of merit. They are for you to discuss, think about, read about and add to. There are of course many other schemes which not only have been recommended but have been carried out by governments.

Can drought be beneficial?

It has been suggested that in some ways drought can be of benefit to the land and people. In economic terms, although the landholders lose money, other people make money. Pastoralists sell fodder, contractors hire out livestock transporters and replacement livestock are sold to those affected by a drought.

Ecologically it seems that droughts can be beneficial to the natural vegetation in preventing the continuing destruction by livestock. A few years without cattle or sheep, or with much-reduced numbers may allow regeneration of natural grasses and bushes. A particular local effect was seen in 1903 when a drought wiped out most of the rabbits of western N.S.W.

Droughts have possibly been the main stimulus for large-scale government finance for rural areas. The setting up of irrigation projects, the building of 'beef roads', and the initiation of water-conservation programmes have been encouraged by periodic droughts. After major droughts there have been millions of dollars spent by governments. Some of this has been used for capital improvement schemes which have long-term benefits.

◀ Fig 6.2 (Photo: The News & Sunday Mail)

Africa, 1968-?

South of the Sahara Desert lies the marginal zone, sometimes called the Sahel, which has supported groups of nomads and settled agriculturalists and herders. Over fifty million people were living in this zone. The map of *isohyets* (lines connecting points of equal rainfall) shows the average rainfall as it appeared to be before the present time. However, since 1968, a continuous drought has gradually devastated the area. In fact, climatologists have traced a decrease in rainfall since 1960.

At the time of writing the drought is still continuing. The Senegal and Niger Rivers have fallen to their lowest levels this century, and Lake Chad has evaporated to one-third its normal size. Fishing villages on its shores, which relied on the lake for food, have been left over 20 km from the water's edge. The coffee and cocoa crops and the peanut harvests are severely reduced, and only a small number of the animals, which provided many nomadic herdsmen with their food, survived.

The drought has most badly hit Mali, Mauritania, Senegal, Upper Volta, Niger, Chad (the Sahel states) and Ethiopia. In Ethiopia the sad story is that many of the deaths could have been prevented. During 1972 the drought had reached a point where widespread starvation was imminent,

◄ Fig 6.3 Father and son collect leaves to eat, Niger 1974. (Photo: Nick Fogden, OXFAM)

Fig 6.4 Drought-stricken Africa 1968–74.

but provincial officials refused to inform the capital city and the Emperor of this. They feared that the information would anger and embarrass Emperor Haile Selassie and that they might be removed from their positions of power.

It was not until the middle of 1973 that the world began to hear of the starvation and suffering in Ethiopia, and even then it was thought to be confined to small pockets of the country. As aid began to trickle in, the Government surveys and relief teams discovered the widespread nature of the famine. It has been estimated that 100 000 people have died in the famine in Ethiopia, but this is only an estimate because population records are not reliable.

In the Sahel states, another 100 000 deaths from the drought have been estimated. In Mali, where livestock are considered more valuable than money, 1 000 000 of the country's 5 000 000 cattle have died.

One of the major effects of the drought has been to displace the nomadic people of the sub-Saharan areas from their traditional wandering areas. The proud Tuareg nomads have tried to overcome the effects of the drought by moving southwards, deserting their usual camps and gathering on the outskirts of towns which can provide some food and water. In these refugee camps, monthly rations of 11 kg of flour and 2 kg of dried milk are being provided. However, the

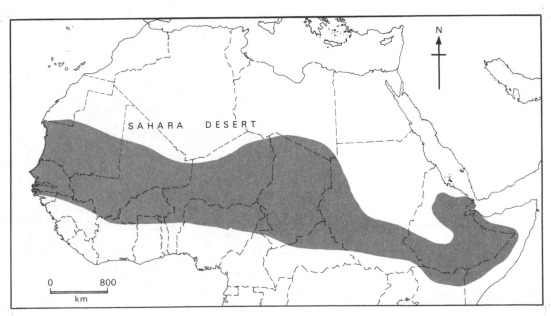

lack of nutritional value in this diet has allowed the spread of disease through the camps. Typhus, measles, dysentery, gastroenteritis and, in some areas cholera, have spread through the refugee camps.

Relief operations

Although the world has only recently understood the magnitude of the disaster caused by the drought, relief is now being sent. In 1973, 518 000 tonnes of grain were delivered, and in 1974, 770 000 tonnes were sent.

The problem of inefficiency in distribution of aid soon became apparent. Some of the grain was sold at a huge profit by local officials, some was left on the docks, but even with the right intentions it was difficult for relief organizations or governments to transport it to the worst areas. Lack of roads and lack of trucks proved an insurmountable barrier.

■ ACTIVITY

1 Find out more about the African drought from newspapers and magazines. What recent developments have occurred in Ethiopia?
2 What are the problems in getting aid to starving people in an area of famine?
3 What effects of the African drought might be long-term? (Some are mentioned in the text.)

Fig 6.5 A once-nomadic Tuareg herdsman proudly shows the millet crop he has grown. (Photo: Nick Fogden, OXFAM)

Is the climate changing?

Until recently, significant changes in climate were only regarded as possible over geological time (millions of years or longer). People who talked about changes within their own lifetime were dismissed as fanciful and forgetful.

However, investigations by meteorologists and climatologists and experts in related fields have now established that there are changes in climate over smaller time periods. They have come to the conclusion that the 1968–74 drought in Africa was caused by the movement of isohyets southward at about 9 km per year since 1960, while in the period 1926–61 the movement was only 1 km per year. From this they have predicted that rain in the Sahelian zone could be 50 per cent of the 1930 total in the year 2030.

Since the 1950s other climatic changes have been noted. Europe and North America have experienced severer winters than before. The tropics are wetter, as are the areas of the Mediterranean and North Africa. North West India is drier, and the southern and western fringes of the Australian desert are wetter.

The climatologists investigating climatic patterns in the last thousand years have established that in the first fifty years of this century, the temperatures in many areas of the world were generally higher than they had been in most earlier times. They say that now we are entering a period of lower temperatures and changes in the rainfall patterns over wide areas.

What has caused this change? Climatologists have put forward various theories, many of them very complex. However, the simplest generally accepted reason seems to be a change in the *circumpolar vortex*, a ring of high altitude winds moving from west to east between 30° and 60° latitude. The circumpolar vortex occurs in both hemispheres, but in the north it appears to have expanded and shifted south since 1960 (fig 6.6). Its southward shift has prevented the monsoons from penetrating to their usual extent northward, limiting rain to Northern India. The penetration of rain to the sub-Saharan zone has also been limited, causing major droughts. There has been a general cooling in the Northern Hemisphere as

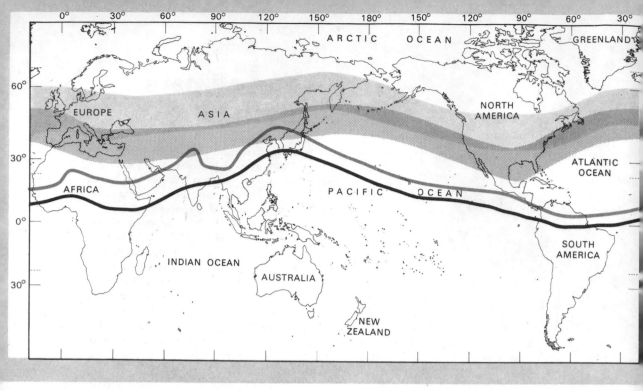

 Circumpolar vortex boundary during recent warm decades

Circumpolar vortex boundary during present cool period

Northern limit of monsoon in recent warm decades

Northern limit of monsoon present cool period

Fig 6.6 The above map shows the substantial change in weather patterns recorded over the past decades. The crucial point is this: is the change a freak fluctuation in a basically stable pattern, or does it represent a major, long-term shift?

the climate belts have migrated southward.

Not all climatologists agree about climatic change. There are a number who say that recorded changes over ten or fifty years are only minor variations, similar to yearly weather differences. They can produce statistics for certain areas which show that climatic patterns are the same in the 1970s as they were in the 1870s. Certainly, the information we have on possible climatic changes is limited, but it indicates distinct trends in climatic change in some areas. Research continuing at the moment may indicate whether or not the climate of the whole earth is changing.

■ ACTIVITY

1   Do people think that the climate of your area is changing? Interview some people over sixty years old and ask for their opinions and the reasons.
2   Are the opinions of people supported by statistical evidence? Try to obtain temperature and rainfall statistics for your area for the last 100 years. Graph the annual rainfall and temperature for each year, and describe any trends that are apparent. Do they support the opinions you have collected?

7 FIRE

ASH ROAD

Ivan Southall

An extract from the novel

He roared into the forest with his headlights on and with the speedometer on fifty. He knew every turn of the road like the back of his hand, knew every rise and every dip. He had pushed vehicles along this road for more than forty years; he had driven horse-carts over it when it had been a track full of pot-holes and ridges. More often than not he traversed it in perfect safety without a conscious memory of having observed a single foot of it. That was how he drove now, at a far higher speed than a man of superior vision would have dared, unaware of what passed him by, except gloom and eerie glow and random shafts of sunlight and the gothic arch of the tall timber through which he rushed.

Wallace and Harry were aware of other things; Wallace of the heat, of the smoke-laden air that sometimes made him cough, of the sheer excitement of an apparent race against time, of the dimness ahead and the blur of the road, and of Harry sitting tensely and precariously on the edge of the back seat with the extremities of his safety-belt barely meeting at the clasp, and with his right hand closed over the sick man's shoulder. Harry's feelings went deeper than impressions, they went straight to questions. Why was the road deserted? Why was there smoke without fire? Where was the fire, for the heat was such that it could have been the blast from an oven thrown open? Was it that the fire upwind was so vast and so widespread that heat went everywhere before it like dragon's breath?

Gramps's voice intruded suddenly. 'Wind up the windows! Jump to it!'

It was the voice of command, and their hands leapt to obey. Then they saw flames to the right, flames at tree-top height exploding like surf on rocks: waves of flame, torrents of flame, flames spraying in fragments, in thousands of pieces, in flaring leaves and twigs that rained on to the road in a storm of fire. It was upon them in seconds, or they had come upon it so swiftly that there was no turning from it: no time to turn, no chance to turn, no place to turn... His lungs felt that they would burst, and his senses swam, and the thin white line began to wander and wobble, and he knew he was going to lose it, he knew that it was going to get away from him, and in panic he touched the brakes.

Instantly he lost the line. It vanished. He didn't know whether it had gone to his left or his right, and the smoke was as dense as a fog, and his tyres were squealing, scorching rubber sliding on bitumen. He felt the change from hard surface to loose surface, from sealed surface to the gravel at the side of the road. In that moment the car struck the bank side-on and spun.

Twice more the car struck the bank, first tail on, then head on; then it stopped.

Acknowledgement: Ivan Southall and Angus & Robertson Publishers for this extract from *Ash Road*.
Fig 7.0 (Photo: Don Stephens & Associations)

Bushfires - generation and spread

The term 'bushfire' is used commonly in Australia for any uncontrolled fire burning through vegetation in the open air. In other areas of the world they may be separated into forest fires, scrub fires or grass fires depending on the type of vegetation.

A fire is only generated under three conditions. There must be heat, oxygen and fuel. The heat must be enough to ignite inflammable material. Common causes of bushfires in Australia are burning off (where small fires get out of control), cigarettes and matches, lightning, campfires and motor vehicles.

The fuel necessary for a bushfire is only present in 40 per cent of the area of Australia. The map of fire-risk seasons (fig 7.1) shows the variation throughout Australia, due to seasonal differences in vegetation growth.

The south-eastern half of Australia, in particular, has one of the world's worst fire risks, due to the combination of climate and vegetation. The area is subject to long, hot summers with periods of hot, dry, northerly winds blowing from the interior of the continent. In summer seasons, after low winter rainfall, there is a lack of subsoil moisture and a drying out of the leaves, branches, bark and grass. Even living trees are partly dried out. This combination of fuel and climate in summer and autumn creates major bushfires every year.

Bushfires can usefully be classed into three main kinds:

Surface fires are those which burn in grass, low shrubs and plant debris (fallen bark and leaves). Many fires start as surface fires. They may travel at a high speed but are relatively easy to control.

Fig 7.2 Surface fire.

Fig 7.1 Seasons of fire risk in Australia.

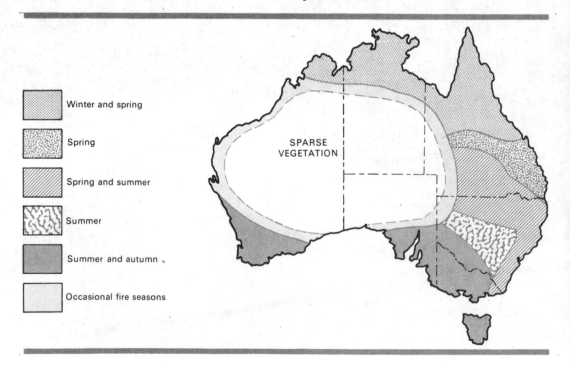

Winter and spring

Spring

Spring and summer

Summer

Summer and autumn

Occasional fire seasons

SPARSE VEGETATION

Dependent crown fires occur when heat and flames from the surface ignite the *crowns* (upper branches and leaves) of trees. The fire in the crowns travels at the same speed as the fire on the surface below.

Fig 7.3 Dependent crown fire.

Running crown fires only occur under conditions of strong, hot winds and very dry vegetation. However, they can be the most devastating fires. The fire in the crowns of the trees progresses ahead of the surface fire and can spread very fast. Pieces of burning vegetation may be carried upwards and outwards by strong convection currents and winds, causing new unpredictable outbreaks (*spot fires*). Burning material carried by these currents has been known to cause fires 8 km ahead of the main front.

Fig 7.4 Running crown fire.

The direction and shape of the spread of bushfires is influenced by a number of factors. Obviously wind is of major importance. Its strength, direction and variability are all critical factors. The type of fuel is also important. If there is an irregular distribution of vegetation types through the path of a fire, the fire will spread at different rates. Even the same type of vegetation may vary in inflammability. Areas of it may be drier or denser than others. Topography and slope have an important influence. When a fire is burning uphill, heat transfer by convection and radiation is increased. Consequently the rate of spread is faster than that on a downslope or level ground.

The extinction of a bushfire relies on removing one of the three necessary conditions (heat, oxygen and fuel). The heat can be lowered by pumping water onto the fuel. The supply of oxygen can be cut off by beating the flames or covering the fuel with earth. The fire can be starved of fuel by creating fire-breaks or pushing in the edge of the fire.

Fire-fighters generally use a combination of these methods, depending on the type of fire and terrain. From years of experience, methods of attack have been worked out for various types of fires. In small fires the advancing head can be attacked and halted, but in larger fires, it is often necessary to work from the flanks of the fire, putting these under control first. The main advance can then be stopped by burning fire-breaks ahead of it.

In Australia and other fire hazard areas there is continual research being conducted into new methods of fire-fighting. Some fire-prevention and control methods are shown on pages 95 and 96.

Hobart, 1967

The background

In southern Tasmania, 1964 and 1965 brought mild winters with below-average rainfall and hot summers. In the autumn and winter of 1966 there were good rains which allowed heavy growth of thick and long grass. More good rains in the spring gave the best season for seven years. At the end of the year a spell of hot weather dried out the growth and the soil. Thus there was a thick coverage of dead grass and dried-out bushes and trees.

Farmers burned off areas of unwanted feed and vegetation. They were accustomed to lighting small fires which burned restricted areas, often being extinguished by rain. Thus throughout January small fires caused by burning-off or clearing were common. In early February, a pall of smoke hung around the hills of the farming districts near Hobart and there were many fire-calls when local fires got out of hand. Extinguishing rain did not come.

February 7th

There had been no rain for ten days and the Bureau of Meteorology forecast a maximum of 31°C with gusty northerlies for the day. However the temperature rose to 39°C and the northerlies came at 40 to 50 knots, hot and dry.

At 3.40 a.m., a fire thought to be safe flared again near Fern Tree. It jumped a road at 6 a.m., spreading and later linking with other fires.

At Magra, gale winds blew a fire towards New Norfolk, where primary school children were herded into a swimming pool for protection. The fire swept on to Boyer destroying a newsprint mill, and then to Dromedary, Bridgewater, Old Beach and then across a 400 metre river to the City of Glenorchy and the suburbs of Hobart.

Fires burst on Hobart from all directions. The outer suburbs penetrated into bushland on the foothills, and the fire rushed down through the forests, exploding on the houses in suburban streets. Telephone services were cut by fire, impeding the emergency communications. The Metropolitan Fire Brigade was overwhelmed by the sudden 'fire-storm' on all sides of the city.

Throughout the day fires spread from other areas, joined together and were blown by the gusting winds.

The town of Snug was almost obliterated, with the death of eleven people there. The Cascade Brewery in Hobart, the convict ruins at Port Arthur and the Carbide factory at Electrona were destroyed or damaged. The map shows the spread of the fires through the area.

The aftermath

The official summing up by insurance firms showed :

62 people dead
1400 houses and major buildings destroyed
1000 farm holdings damaged
50 000 sheep killed
300 dairy cattle killed
25 000 laying hens lost
10% of the State's reserves of fodder lost
5% of pasture land burned
80 bridges destroyed or damaged
$15 million of insurance paid out.

◄ Fig 7.5 Fire-blackened ruins in Hobart, February 1967. (Photo: Don Stephens & Associates)

Fig 7.6 Pattern of the Hobart fire.

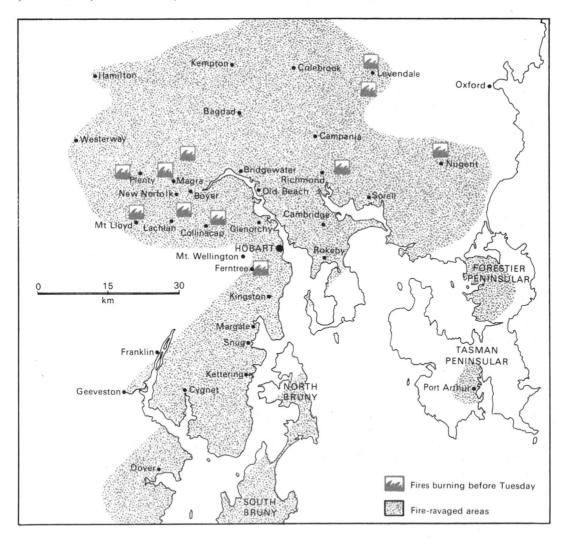

Why did it happen?

There was a combination of meteorological, locational and human factors which led to the situation.

The maximum temperature in Hobart on February 7th was 39.3°C, the highest this century. The relative humidity was 12 per cent. Winds averaged 45 knots but gusted to 70 knots. There had been no rain for 10 days and only 12 mm since January 1st, in contrast to the average of 42 mm. Since November there had been 50 mm in contrast to the average of 150 mm.

Hobart, unlike the more northerly cities of Melbourne and Adelaide, had rarely experienced major bushfires. People living near bushland in the outer suburbs took no fire precautions. The suburbs had gradually spread into the hilly bushland without small bushfires making the people conscious of potential danger.

Farmers burned off excess grass and relied on rains to extinguish the fires if they started to spread. Even the fires which spread into forest were tolerated by fire authorities who knew that rain was the most effective extinguisher in areas difficult of access.

In the week before February 7th, reports of up to fourteen fires a day were common. Fires were beaten away from the back fences of houses in the outer suburbs and fires burned continuously in the mountains ringing Hobart. On Saturday and Sunday the 4th and 5th February, twenty fires destroyed thousands of hectares of forest and grazing land.

Hobart was a fire trap due to the combination of climatic and locational features, but it was the apathy towards possible catastrophe which was the main ingredient of the disaster.

■ DISCUSSION

Do you agree or disagree with the conclusion, outlined above, on the cause of Hobart's fire tragedy?

■ ACTIVITY

Assess your local area for potential fire hazard. Draw up a list of dangers. Could a fire spread from one house or backyard to another? Read carefully the details on fires and their spread while you are doing this.

Clare, 1965 - a rural bushfire

Most of the bushfires which occur in Australia affect only the rural areas. It is the occasional fire which reaches the outskirts of city areas, such as the Blue Mountains, the Dandenongs or the Adelaide Hills, which tends to get most publicity.

An examination of one rural fire can be valuable in showing some general characteristics. A fire near Clare in the mid-north of South Australia has been chosen because it has been studied in detail.

On February 21st, the meteorological conditions over the mid-north of South Australia suggested high fire danger. The air temperature was 40°C, relative humidity was 10 per cent, wind speed was 15 to 25 knots and coming from the north-north-west. During the day the high surface temperatures caused instability in the atmosphere, with much turbulence.

The fire started at 1.55 p.m. in dry grass on a vacant block on the southern outskirts of Clare. It swept southwards through undulating savannah woodland country interspersed with orchards and vineyards. The savannah woodland was made up of stands of blue gum (Eucalyptus Leucoxylon), some native pine (Callitris) and shrubs including hopbush (Dodonea).

The location of vineyards south of the town split the fire, after about ten minutes, into two separate prongs. Each of the prongs of fire nearly extinguished themselves by coming against vineyards and roads, but high grass along fence lines helped their spread. In fact it was the high and dense grass along fence lines which allowed the fire to spread to unexpected places.

In the first three hours the fire spread along a narrow front south-eastwards toward Mintaro. The map (fig 7.7) shows the pattern and the three tables on page 93 should be consulted with the map.

The Bureau of Meteorology forecast a cool change during the day. This is the typical progression of a cold front over southern Australia, with a change from a northerly to a south-westerly wind.

Fig 7.7 How change in wind direction affected the Clare fire. ▶

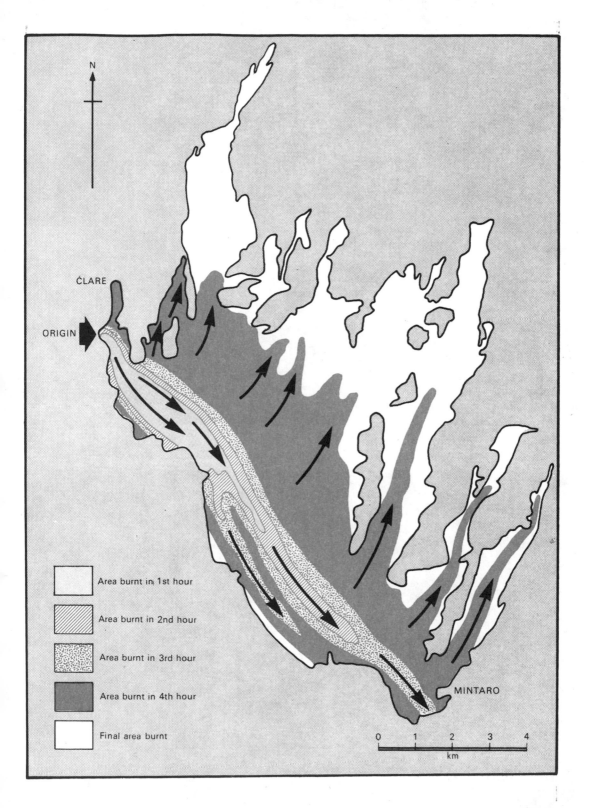

N

CLARE

ORIGIN

Area burnt in 1st hour

Area burnt in 2nd hour

Area burnt in 3rd hour

Area burnt in 4th hour

Final area burnt

MINTARO

0   1   2   3   4
km

Fig 7.8 Some homesteads miraculously escaped the Clare fire.

Fig 7.9 Others were destroyed, although in apparently safer positions. (Photos: Bushfire Research Committee of S.A.)

At 5 p.m. the wind change came, bringing gusty south-west winds reaching 35 knots. The eastern flank of the fire, about 12 km long, flared again and the fire spread over the undulating cropping and grazing farmland. It was this wind change which caused the most damage. Previously the small front had seemed controllable, but now the wide front trebled the area burnt in one hour.

The perimeter of the fire is of course most important to fire fighting because it is the distance over which the fire must be extinguished, mopped up and patrolled. Table 2 shows the sudden increase of the problem after the wind change.

The fire fighting was done by twenty volunteer E.F.S. (Emergency Fire Services of S.A.) appliances and crews, aided by some privately owned fire units. They were in constant radio contact with the Fire Supervisor but had problems with access to properties and to water sources. In some places windmills and tanks had collapsed because the fire had burnt out wooden supports. In other places there was a lack of signposts on intersections which confused fire units from other areas and the poor condition of council roads caused loss of valuable time for the fire units.

Recommendations by the Bushfire Protection Officer

A detailed investigation led to the mapping of the fire and the calculation of the tables shown. The following recommendations apply to any rural area where there is danger of bushfire.

1 Trees and shrubs should not be so close as to spread the fire to a building or to prevent easy access by firefighters.

2 Fly-wire screens on windows, doors and ventilators can prevent wind-borne burning debris from entering houses and starting fires inside.

3 A safe area of low grass should exist around each house. This can protect the house and provide a herding area for animals in a fire.

4 Grass along fence lines and roadsides should be cleared each summer. Even breaks at strategic points along fence lines would help.

5 More safe areas should be provided for stock, preferably with watering facilities.

6 Hay-sheds with valuable fodder reserves should be positioned south and east of the homestead buildings, within the safe area.

7 Water reticulation systems, such as tanks and windmills, should be fire-resistant structures.

8 Each farm should have well-marked access tracks to water and strategic areas.

■ ACTIVITY

1 Draw graphs to represent the data in tables. Compare the values before and after the wind change, and discuss the problems of wind changes during bushfires.

2 Using the recommendations of the Bushfire Prevention Officer, draw up a map of an imaginary farm property which has all the possible fire precautions. Use distinct colours and symbols in the legend to show the features.

Table 1: Area burnt, hour by hour

Elapsed time (hours)	1	2	3	4	Time of control
Progressive area burnt (hectares)	380	700	1380	4520	8000

Table 2: Fire perimeter, hour by hour

Elapsed time (hours)	1	2	3	4	Time of control
Perimeter (kilometres)	14	24	37	67	114

Table 3: Average rates of forward spread

Period	1st hour	2nd hour	3rd hour	4th hour
Average rates of spread (km/h)	6	4	3–4	5–6

Vegetation and fire in Australia

Large areas of central Australia have vegetation which is too sparse to support a bushfire (fig 7.1). Other areas in the mountains of the east coast are covered with tropical or temperate rainforest which is rarely dry enough for large-scale fires.

Between these two extremes, a large part of Australia has a *sclerophyll* vegetation, where the leaves of trees and bushes are leathery in texture. The dominant trees of the sclerophyll forests are Eucalypts but there is generally an 'understorey' of bushes and shrubs of various kinds.

The Eucalypt species have been found to possess particular fire-resistant characteristics. Many of them are not killed by a fire which completely burns off the crown and smaller branches. Shoots are sent out from the surviving stems in the following season after some species are burned. The buds which can send out these shoots are along the stem and protected from fire by a thick layer of bark.

Other Eucalypts have *lignotubers* (masses of dormant buds and food material) at ground level which can produce new shoots after severe burning of the stem. Trees of the Acacia family often possess fire-resistant seed, another adaptation. Sometimes the seeds lie dormant in the ground for many years and then germinate after a fire.

The sclerophyll vegetation obviously has quite a resistance to fire. Studies of similar climatic areas such as the Mediterranean, California and South Africa have shown similar adaptational characteristics. Studies of forests have shown that bushfires must have been a normal occurrence in the growth of forests long before man came to Australia. Sclerophyll forests in medium rainfall areas apparently had a fire frequency of from three to thirty years. The fires must have been mainly caused by lightning. At present lightning accounts for about 8 per cent of bushfires, but with no men to extinguish them, fires caused by lightning could have spread through thousands of square kilometres. They would have been extinguished eventually by rain or wind changes or exhaustion of the fuel.

In areas where fires occurred frequently the *plant litter* (leaves, bark, dead branches on the ground, etc.) would be burned and would not accumulate. Possibly the fire would only be a surface fire, having insufficient heat to become a crown fire. However, since man has moved into areas near forests and woodland, he has done his best to stop fires. Thus many timbered areas do not experience a fire for perhaps thirty years. By this time the plant litter has built up considerably and provides a substantial load of fuel. A fire which eventually spreads into such an area can burn more fiercely and will almost certainly become a crown fire. The fire will be much more difficult to control and may spread far from its source, causing damage to property and life. In this way the efforts of man in limiting bushfires sometimes has the opposite effect. Instead of frequent but small fires, we may in some areas be causing less frequent but more dangerous fires.

Fire control and prevention

Fig 7.10 A sprinkler system on the roof helps to prevent burning material setting fire to the roof and also cools the exterior, reducing the risk of explosion. (Photo: Advertiser Newspapers Ltd) ▶

Fig 7.11 Water-bombing can be an effective fire-fighting method in rugged, heavily timbered areas. This aircraft, operated by the Quebec Government, is seen dropping its 3500 kg load around the perimeter of a fire.

Fig 7.12 Fire rages through bushland in Victoria. (Photo: Herald & Weekly Times Ltd)

8 LANDSLIDES

Causes of landslides

The basic cause of landslides is gravity. Rocks, soil and debris will fall if they are not supported in some way and the natural form of support is friction. When friction is lessened by one or more factors, a rock mass may become unstable and movement may occur.

Landslides are really only one kind of rock and soil movement which is given the general name of *mass wasting*. A less obvious form of mass wasting is *soil and rock creep*, a slow but widespread movement which is constantly occurring on many slopes. The more rapid mass movements include *earthflows*, *mudflows*, *debris avalanches* and *subsidence*. These are all kinds of landslides.

Here are some of the factors which, individually or together, may cause landslides:

●change of slope gradient, by undermining or excavation
●overloading by building embankments or dumping huge loads of waste
●shocks and vibrations: earthquakes, explosions and vibrations by machines
●changes in water content caused by excess rainfall or melt-water, or by extremely dry conditions
●effects of ground-water exerting pressure or washing out fine particles
●effects of freezing water increasing in volume and widening fissures
●weathering of rocks, gradually breaking up and disturbing the cohesion of the rocks.
●changes in vegetation cover of slopes, causing changes in the water content and stability of slopes.

St Jean Vianney . . .

The town of St Jean Vianney in Canada was given many warnings of impending trouble. Cracks appeared in road surfaces, small areas of land sank a few centimetres, telegraph poles appeared to sway when there was no wind, unusual thumps were heard, and there was a sizeable landslide on a hill nearby. These events prompted the local inhabitants to request soil inspections by the Government.

After several days of heavy rain, on 4 May 1971, one side of Blackburn Hill started to slide and the mass of *lignified clay* (clay formed from decomposed wood) came down towards the town. It seemed as if the earth had dissolved to a depth of thirty metres and flowed as if it were a river down the hill, over part of the town, toward the Saguenay River.

Thirty-eight houses were engulfed and thirty-one people were killed in the mudflow before it settled again. Geologists who investigated the area said

◄ Fig 8.0 A landslide engulfs a mountain village, Japan 1965.

Fig 8.1 Landslide caused by an earthquake, 1968. (Photos: Japanese National Research Centre for Disaster Prevention)

... mudflow

that the landslide could have been triggered by the large-scale erosion at the base of Blackburn Hill or by an earth tremor. However, they also discovered that the whole town had been built on the site of a landslide that occurred about 500 years ago. Therefore the Quebec Government declared the site of the town to be unsafe for future occupation.

In this case, then, reconstruction was done on a new site. Most of the inhabitants of the town wanted to stay together, so they chose land in a location nearby. The Government undertook to build new houses there and to transfer the undamaged houses from the old site. A fund contributed by the people of Canada allowed the families to replace their lost possessions. Thus the survivors of the local disaster were able to continue to have their old neighbours in a similar community to that of the destroyed St Jean Vianney.

■ **DISCUSSION**
1 What action could be taken to prevent disaster after the kind of events preceding the landslide?
2 What actions of the Government would have most pleased the survivors of St Jean Vianney?
3 (a) What actions should a government take after a disaster to minimise the financial losses of survivors?

(b) What actions can a government take to minimise the emotional disturbance to survivors of a disaster?
4 Using your imagination, draw a sketch of the landslide engulfing St Jean Vianney.

Peru - landslide after earthquake

Twenty thousand people were killed in the tourist town of Yungay, Peru, in May 1970 when an earthquake dislodged a mass of rock and ice from the surrounding mountains. One landslide came from the north-east and another came from the south-east face of Mount Huascaran (7300 m). Whole villages were swept away, and the town of Yungay was buried under five metres of mud. The speed of the rock and ice mass was estimated at over 200 km/h.

Because many of the small villages were isolated in the mountains, there were great problems with rescue efforts. Planes operated shuttle services into the disaster area, but there was a lack of co-ordination.

In addition, there were complaints that the rescuers ignored the local native Indian population and used all seats on the planes to rescue relatives of Government officials. Accusations were also made that on the outward journeys soldiers with guns were being carried instead of medicines. The Government argued that the maintenance of law and order was essential. Some overseas doctors who had flown to Peru left after two days, disgusted that they had not been given transport to fly to the disaster area.

Fig 8.2 The Yungay landslide (below) almost covers a new school. (Photo: Philip Jackson, OXFAM)

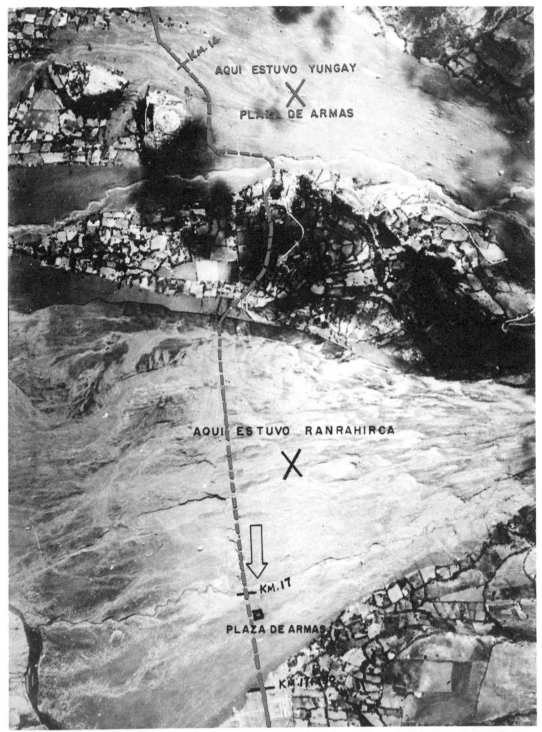

Fig 8.3 Aerial view of the landslide. The dotted line indicates the highway. 'Aqui estuvo Yungay Plaza de Armas' means 'Here was the town square of Yungay'.

Aberfan

In the valleys of Southern Wales dominated by coal mining, the waste material from the underground mines has always been a problem. From fifty years or more of continuous mining, the slag amounts to a massive quantity. The usual solution for the early mine owners was to heap it on the side of the valley, or within the valley. Over the years a sizeable man-made hill formed near many villages.

There were quite a number of small slides of the slag material on various hillsides. In 1939, 180 000 tonnes slipped 0.5 km near Abercynn, and in 1965 there was movement of the large Ty Mawr tip in the Rhondda Valley.

In 1944 and again in 1963, there were small slides in the large slag heap behind the village of Aberfan, and in 1965 a petition was signed by the townspeople who sent it to the Merthyr Borough Council. No action was taken.

In October 1966 there was a week of heavy rain around Aberfan. The slag became saturated and part of it turned into a slurry. As the rain stopped on the October 21st, the layer nearest to the town suddenly slid, pouring over the local primary school. The soggy mass of slag, rock and mud engulfed the whole building, killing 5 teachers and 116 children.

The village had lost most of one generation. This was the way the world and the village people viewed the disaster. Accusations were thrown at the National Coal Board and Borough Council. Although the immediate causes of the slide were natural, the ultimate causes were seen to be man-made.

The National Coal Board defended itself by saying 'the disaster was due to a coincidence of a set of geological factors, each of which in itself is not exceptional but which collectively created a particularly critical geological environment'. However, the official report by the government criticised the Board for paying little attention to its coal-tips. It said that the care the Board had taken over the surveying, planning and dangers of winning the coal, was not extended to the disposal of wastes. There was never a general policy for siting, working and inspecting the tips, and the officials who occasionally inspected them knew

Fig 8.4   The slag-heap above Aberfan. ▲

Fig 8.5 Rescue workers crowd the disaster site. (Photos: Associated Newspapers Ltd) ▼

little of civil engineering and soil mechanics.

The official report stated 'the Aberfan disaster is a terrifying tale of bungling ineptitude by many men charged with tasks for which they were totally unfitted, of failure to heed clear warnings, and of total lack of direction from above'.

Such an outspoken condemnation brought a distinct policy change from the Government and Coal Board towards the coal-tips. Wherever possible, the unsightly heaps were smoothed and planted with grasses and small bushes. This has the dual effect of eliminating danger of slips and improving the appearance of the area.

The village afterwards

Money and aid poured into Aberfan from all over the world. But this created new problems. How do you assess the worth of a child's life in monetary terms? Should money be given to those whose children survived?

The fund for Aberfan brought in $A7.5 million, but this caused arguments and strife within the village. There were complaints at the appointment of a lawyer to administer the fund on a salary of $A8400 a year. There were arguments about the allocation of the money to community projects rather than individual families.

The first distribution of money was to bereaved parents for funeral expenses, holidays away from the village, repairs to damaged houses, and to surviving children. Each bereaved family received $A980 and each family whose child survived $A560. In addition the Coal Board offered $A1400 to each bereaved family. But some bereaved parents were asking for up to $A14 000.

A part of the fund was set aside for surviving children who might show the emotional and mental effects of the tragedy in the future. But adults were already showing these signs. An anonymous letter was sent to one parent, saying 'Why should your child live and mine die?'

A village community centre was planned to use a large amount of the fund for the benefit of all the people. But there were worries that much of the money might remain in the bank while people argued about it.

■ DISCUSSION

1 Was the tragedy natural or man-made?
2 What could have been done to prevent the disaster?

Longarone - landslide and inundation

Longarone is a small town in Northern Italy. In 1960, in the valley above the town, the Vaiont Dam was built. It was the second-highest concrete structure in the world. Before, during and after the building of the dam, landslides in the valley were common. A large one, which fell while the dam was still filling, alerted the local populace to the danger.

Precautions were taken. A line of stakes was placed on the hillsides, and their movement measured every day. An average movement of 25 to 30 cm a week was observed, but this was said to be common on steep hill slopes in the area. Deep holes were bored to investigate the underlying rocks, but these did not reveal any special problems.

However, deeper in the rocks than these bores penetrated, there was a layer of clay and *marl* (an earthy deposit composed of clay and calcium carbonate) below the surface limestone, a layer which was steeply inclined toward the valley. In September 1963, water from a period of exceptionally heavy rainfall penetrated the many joints of the limestone and lubricated the plane of contact between the limestone and the clays.

At 10.43 p.m. on October 9th, several million tonnes of rock slipped down the slope and into the waters of the reservoir. The water displaced by the avalanche of rock rose in a 70-metre wave which rushed across the dam's surface, over the dam wall, down the valley and onto the town of Longarone. Two thousand people were killed and the village engulfed. The dam wall itself remained intact after the water had rushed over it.

Could the disaster have been averted?
There are two separate questions here. We are really asking:
- could the avalanche have been prevented?
- could the loss of life have been prevented?

The avalanche
The geological structure which caused the landslide has been described above. It is obvious that with the lubrication provided by the heavy rains, a landslide at some time was inevitable. But, people in the area knew of the likelihood of landslide. There had been a major one in 1960 when the reservoir was partly filled. The flood wave from this was contained behind the dam wall, but it gave sufficient warning of the danger.

The people reacted by keeping a careful watch on the slopes of Monte Toe, and measuring earth movements. After the disaster, it was shown that the measuring was not extensive enough to give the precise information needed. If the engineers and geologists had known of the layer of clay and marl, perhaps other measures would have been taken.

The loss of life

Even if the avalanche could not have been averted, perhaps the loss of life could have been reduced by relocation of the village. Was there enough evidence to justify this? Some indications of the impending avalanche were given to the local people. The movement of the stakes planted in the hillside increased with the torrential rain, ten days before the avalanche. The pattern of movement had been recorded carefully for three years so that it could be used. Even the animals of the area sensed impending danger (so it was said afterwards) and moved away seven days before the rockfall.

With the accumulation of evidence of the impending rockfall, and the general awareness of the local people of landslides in the area, why was the village not evacuated? Perhaps the remoteness of government authority and the general reluctance of people to alter their daily pattern of living unless disaster has already struck, can explain this in part.

■ ACTIVITY

1 What schemes could have been adopted to prevent the massive landslide of 1963? Should the dam have been sited in an area prone to rock falls? What other information would be needed before you could decide on this?

2 Refer to the section on landslide control (page 106). Comment on the use of these methods for the prevention of this landslide.

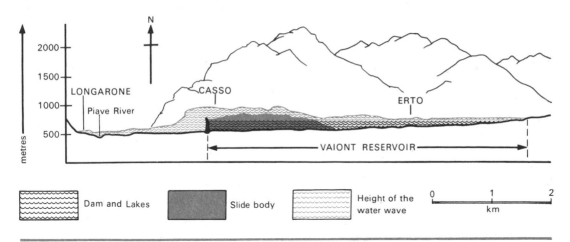

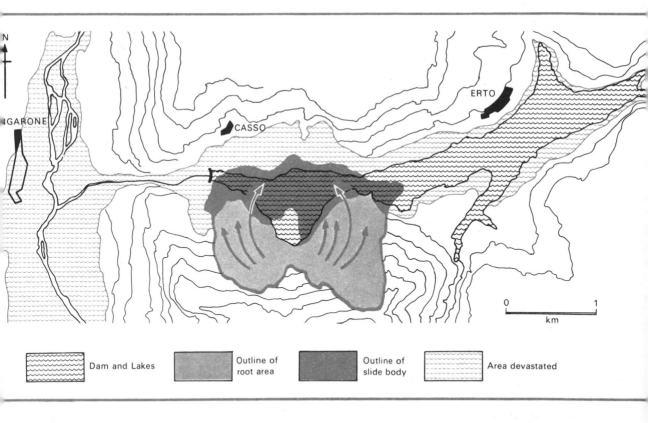

Fig 8.6 Longitudinal profile of the Vaiont valley.

Fig 8.7 Contour map showing the dam, the root area of the landslide and the area devastated.

Landslide prevention methods

In any area which has experienced landslides or where there is a likelihood of them happening, some of the following actions may be carried out. It must be emphasised that any one plan is not as simple as it may appear here in a straightforward list of methods. A well-thought-out plan should tackle tasks in order of urgency so that one does not interfere with another.

■ METHODS

1 Treatment of the slope shape by lowering the top or enlarging the base may increase stability.
2 Drainage of the surface may remove the lubricating agent.
3 Drainage of the sub-surface ground water by boring and pumping can be effective if it follows geological research.
4 Planting landslides with vegetation can aid the drying out of surface layers and consolidate them with a network of roots.
5 Retaining walls are used in some areas to protect railways or to anchor the base of a slope.
6 Rock bolts, similar to those used in mining and tunnelling, have been applied successfully to areas of suitable rock.
7 Hardening of the soils by the use of electricity, heat and cement has been used on a small scale.
8 A temporary method, not altogether reliable, is the use of blasting to break the slip surface. This may cause a number of smaller controlled landslides instead of a large, destructive landslide.

Practical simulation of landslides

■ ACTIVITY

In a sand tray or any suitable outdoor area, try the following experiments:
1 Using sand, clay (powdered and in lumps), river gravel, blue-metal chips and loam, pour some of each material from a height of 20 cm on to the tray. Note the steepness of the slopes formed by each material. Measure the angle of each and sketch them. Try the same experiment with wet materials. What reasons can you give for the results?
2 Cover a board with a thin layer of powdered clay. Place a brick on the board and raise one end of the board until the brick slides off. Measure the angle of the board's slope at this point. Now wet the powdered clay and repeat the experiment. What differences are noted?
3 Build a slope on a base-board using a mixture of the materials listed above, placing them in uneven layers or pockets. Place a small weight or object (to represent a house) on the side of a slope. Vibrate the base-board with increasing force. What changes occur in the slope and the position of the house?
4 Undermine the slope a little at its base and repeat the vibrations. Which materials (or which layers or pockets) are least affected by the vibration?

9 FREEZES
AND AVALANCHES

Freeze-ups

The earth's atmosphere is in a state of continuous change. We talk about the daily changes in atmospheric conditions as 'weather'. Occasionally there are deviations from the usual pattern in the form of freeze-ups, droughts and heat-waves.

The photograph of snow-bound New York (fig 9.0) shows the effects of abnormally cold conditions. In winter densely populated areas are sometimes subject to prolonged periods of severe cold and heavy snowfalls. This disrupts the normal pattern of life, blocks roads, closes airports and freezes water-pipes. In the case of a sudden thaw, there is the danger of flooding.

Freeze-ups such as this occur when a mass of air from polar regions penetrates to the middle latitudes. Usually, such polar air masses warm up as they travel towards the equator, but occasionally there is a large, cold-air mass which retains its characteristics. These are known as *polar outbreaks*. The very cold air in the upper levels causes snow to form and may produce an intense low-pressure system and accompanying high winds. Heavy snowfalls combined with strong winds create blizzard conditions which may seriously affect a wide area.

The polar air masses may remain over one area for a number of days or they may move to a new area. The longer the air mass remains in a temperate area, the warmer it becomes. But for the first few days in particular, its effect may be quite dramatic.

Fig 9.0 New York brought to a standstill. (Photo: Advertiser Newspapers Ltd)

The Ice Age

Changes in the atmosphere also take place on a much longer time scale than daily changes in weather. Over millions of years there have been great variations in the world's climatic pattern.

The last great fall in temperature coincided with the spread of early man to Europe. About 700 000 years before the present (B.P.) the temperature of the atmosphere fell, allowing snow and ice to accumulate and spread towards the Equator. This was the most recent Ice Age, in the Pleistocene era. The temperature rose and fell, and the ice retreated and advanced for over 600 000 years. About 10 000 years B.P. the temperature steadily rose, ending the Ice Age.

There has been a great amount of investigation into the causes of the Ice Age. Research has so far only revealed possible theories. Some theories suggested variations in the energy output of the sun as the cause, others an increase in dust in the atmosphere filtering solar radiation and so reducing the surface temperature. The possibility of changes in the tilt of the earth's axis have also been investigated. It seems that whatever was the original stimulus, the presence of large areas of ice over the northern continents lowered the atmospheric temperature further and so hindered precipitation.

The Ice Age was made up of a series of advances and retreats of the ice. Evidence points to there being four main glacial advances within the Pleistocene era, separated by interglacial periods.

By 500 000 B.P. early man had spread to Europe. As the ice advanced from the north, forests shrank. Over thousands of years man retreated to the Mediterranean area.

During the great interglacial period, of about 100 000 years duration, groups of men settled by the sea, rivers and lakes, spreading northward. They hunted large animals in the temperate forests. But as the ice advanced again, the descendants of these men were forced to move to Mediterranean areas and North Africa for food gathering. A short interglacial period brought warm temperatures allowing another spread northward migration.

The group of early men whom we know as *Neanderthal Man* had developed adaptations to cold conditions by the time of the last glaciation. They sheltered in caves, used fire for warmth, and dressed themselves in skins. Thus they were able to stay in the areas of increasing cold, rather than retreating to the south. There was a time of improved climate during the last glacial period and *Cro-Magnon Man* showed further development and availability of leisure by painting the walls of caves and engraving bone and ivory. The richness of animal life and ease of food-getting allowed this.

After the final retreat of the glaciers (about 10 000 B.P.), deciduous and mixed forests developed over much of Europe. Bows and arrows were developed by post-glacial man, and the skills of hunting were developed until 5000 B.P. when the skills of agriculture and herding of domesticated animals spread from the East.

The knowledge which we possess about the Ice Age is made up of many small pieces of information which have been interpreted in different ways. The process of discovering new facts and fitting them with others is still continuing. The knowledge that we do possess shows an interesting pattern of man's response to the glacial periods. The development of new skills and knowledge during the Ice Age allowed later man to remain in the cold regions rather than follow his ancestors in retreating to the south.

■ DISCUSSION

1 Do you think that the Ice Age should be included as a 'natural disaster'? Is the duration of time your only objection?

2 Find out more about Neanderthal and Cro-Magnon Man.

3 What kind of creatures did early man hunt during the Ice Age? Distinguish between animals of the glacial and interglacial period.

AVALANCHE!

A. Rutgers Van der Loeff

*An extract from the book
translated from the Dutch by Dora Round*

And then it happened. In the middle of the night. Just below the top of the Kühelihorn a great mass of snow broke loose with a crash like an explosion. Slowly it began to shift, it seemed to hesitate, but only for a little. A few seconds later the avalanche hurtled down, its path growing wider and wider, the force of the air driven before it blasting the village even before the thundering mass leapt upon the snow-covered houses and sheds like a wild beast. It lasted a far shorter time than anyone could have believed. One moment the village was safe and sound and fast asleep. The next, a great hole was torn in it. Part of it was still buried so deep in snow and wrapped in such deceptive silence that an onlooker would never have guessed the terrible thing that had happened. But part of it, even beyond the path of the avalanche, had houses blown down by blast, walls swept away, shutters and window frames ripped off and smashed...

Oil lamps were lit in houses here and there, light shone through cracks and through the patterns cut in the shutters. Men with lighted torches clambered over the shapeless mounds of snow, which were strewn with wreckage. More and more people started calling to each other. There was a sound of hysterical sobbing. Men shouted orders to each other. The dim beams of electric torches were pointed helplessly at the huge misshapen masses of snow from which protruded broken bits of wood, smashed crockery, the wheels of a pram, the leg of a chair, torn rags of stuff and ripped-off pieces of balcony. It was a chaotic sight which struck people speechless as they looked at it. One of them sobbed. Most of them stood about dumbly in the flickering light of the torches.

'The wind's changed,' said someone.

'Yes, the wind's changed,' someone else answered dully.

The changing wind, the falling snow, the towering mountains, high and pitiless, what can man do against them?..

The heart of the village had never been threatened in the memory of man. The villagers had feared for the outlying parts, where perhaps more houses had been built during the last few decades than was prudent in view of the known path of the avalanches. But they had taken all measures to ensure their safety.

The snow-breaks and fences, the barriers and trenches had all been under deep snow for days. The villagers had been anxious about the safety of the outlying houses, and with reason. But avalanches have sudden whims which leave one speechless with astonishment. The avalanche from the Kühelihorn had taken a totally unexpected route, one which it had never followed before. It had struck the very place where people believed themselves safest...

Acknowledgement: A. Rutgers Van der Loeff, Dorothy Round (translator) and Brockhampton Press Ltd for this extract from *Avalanche*!

◄Fig 9.1 (Photo: Eidg. Institut für Schnee-und Lawinenforschung Weissfluhjoch)

Avalanches

An avalanche occurs when a mass of snow on a mountainside loses its hold and falls. Sometimes avalanches are divided into two categories — the *ground avalanche* of wet snow, which slides over the ground carrying stones and debris with it, and the *powder avalanche*, consisting of dry, powdery snow. But there are many combinations of these two kinds of avalanche.

Snow may be anchored on mountain sides by irregularities, such as rock outcrops. The structure of layers within the snow is important. The angle of slope is also obviously significant, but wet snow has been known to slide on a 15° slope and hard snow can hold on a 50° slope.

Vibrations of some sort usually begin an avalanche. Earthquakes of course can cause major avalanches. The falling of a tree, perhaps under pressure from snow, or the progress of an animal or man are other causes. The vibrations from trains are also a cause of many avalanches.

The pressures exerted by the falling snow can be very great. Further destruction is often caused by an explosion of compressed air which has been trapped by the falling snow. When snow falls almost vertically, the compressed air underneath may burst out like a bomb blast. When the slope is not so steep, the air is pushed ahead of the avalanche as a strong wind. In other avalanches the air trapped inside the falling snow bursts out while it is travelling. Thus, in many avalanches, the trapped or 'exploding' air may cause as much damage as the falling snow.

(1) From single point	(2) From large area leaving wall
LOOSE-SNOW AVALANCHE	SLAB AVALANCHE
(3) Whole snow cover involved	(4) Some top strata only involved
FULL DEPTH AVALANCHE	SURFACE AVALANCHE
(5) Open slope	(6) In a gully
UNCONFINED AVALANCHE	CHANNELLED AVALANCHE

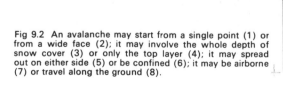
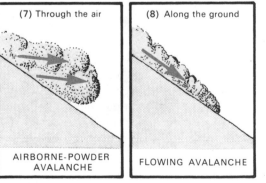

(7) Through the air — AIRBORNE-POWDER AVALANCHE

(8) Along the ground — FLOWING AVALANCHE

Fig 9.2 An avalanche may start from a single point (1) or from a wide face (2); it may involve the whole depth of snow cover (3) or only the top layer (4); it may spread out on either side (5) or be confined (6); it may be airborne (7) or travel along the ground (8).

Switzerland - winter of 1950-51

Although avalanches occur every year in valleys scattered through the Alps, the winter of 1950–51 produced avalanches which affected almost every part of the Alps. The set of conditions responsible for this began with the build-up of a frontal system over the Alps. Warm, moist air was moving north-eastwards from Spain, meeting cold air from Germany and the North Sea, which forced the warm air to rise. The warm air cooled as it rose, causing huge cumulonimbus storm clouds which produced heavy falls of snow. The centre of the storms developed over north-east Switzerland in the middle of January 1951, and the blizzards continued for three weeks.

One village which was partly destroyed was Airolo. During the storms of January, 200 people had been evacuated because of danger from the 'Vallascia', a ravine above the village. When snowing stopped on February 7th, most people returned to their homes, but snowing started again on February 10th.

On February 11th, an avalanche came down the slopes on the opposite side to the Vallascia, and the village was evacuated again. A few houses near the main street were exempted from the order because no avalanche had ever reached so far as the main street. The storm continued throughout the day and night, producing two small avalanches. The villagers kept watch from safe positions.

At five minutes past midnight the Vallascia avalanche came down. Two gusts of wind hit the village followed by a long deep rumble and a crash. An estimated volume of 500 000 tonnes of wet snow had fallen. It reached right to the main street (fig 9.3), destroying both evacuated and occupied houses. Some people had disobeyed official instructions and returned to their houses, and these were among the ten people killed by the avalanche. Twenty-nine buildings were damaged or destroyed.

This was only one village affected by avalanches in the winter of 1950–51. In the Swiss, Austrian and Italian Alps, 700 people were killed, and 2500 buildings were destroyed.

Fig 9.3 Avalanche at Airolo, 1951. (Photo: Institut für Schnee- und Lawinenforschung Weissflujoch)

Protection from avalanches

This picture essay shows some of the methods of protection against avalanche. Much of the research for this has been done by the Swiss Federal Institute for Snow and Avalanche Research. This organization, based at Davos in the Swiss Alps, came into being in 1942. There are five divisions working on climatology and snowfall, snow mechanics, vegetation and reafforestation, physics of snow and ice, and formation of snow and hail. Because the Institute is on a steep slope, and has itself been subjected to avalanches, it is very close to the immediate problems of avalanches.

Fig 9.4 Anti-avalanche barrages.

Fig 9.5 Protective gallery tunnel over the road at Tremola in the Swiss Alps.

Fig 9.6 The village of Andermatt has been protected by planting a forest on the slopes above it.

Fig 9.7 This church at Oberwald has bows like a ship, designed to lessen the shock of an avalanche. (Photos: Swiss National Tourist Office, Zürich)

Fig 9.4

Fig 9.5

Fig 9.6

Fig 9.7

Fig 9.8 Dogs have been specially trained to locate and dig out people buried by avalanches. (Photo: Swiss National Tourist Office, Zürich)

10 DISEASE

A JOURNAL OF THE PLAGUE YEAR
Daniel Defoe

An extract from the book

One of the worst days we had in the whole time, as I thought, was in the beginning of September, when, indeed, good people began to think that God was resolved to make a full end of the people in this miserable city. This was at that time when the plague was fully come into the eastern parishes. The parish of Aldgate, if I may give my opinion, buried above a thousand a week for two weeks, though the bills did not say so many; — but it surrounded me at so dismal a rate that there was not a house in twenty uninfected in the Minories, in Houndsditch, and in those parts of Aldgate parish about the Butcher Row and the alleys over against me. I say, in those places death reigned in every corner. Whitechapel parish was in the same condition, and though much less than the parish I lived in, yet buried near 600 a week by the bills, and in my opinion near twice as many. Whole families, and indeed whole streets of families, were swept away together; insomuch that it was frequent for neighbours to call to the bellman to go to such-and-such houses and fetch out the people, for that they were all dead.

And, indeed, the work of removing the dead bodies by carts was now grown so very odious and dangerous that it was complained of that the bearers did not take care to clear such houses where all the inhabitants were dead, but that sometimes the bodies lay several days unburied, till the neighbouring families were offended with the stench, and consequently infected; and this neglect of the officers was such that the churchwardens and constables were summoned to look after it, and even the justices of the Hamlets were obliged to venture their lives among them to quicken and encourage them, for innumerable of the bearers died of the distemper, infected by the bodies they were obliged to come so near. And had it not been that the number of poor people who wanted employment and wanted bread (as I have said before) was so great that necessity drove them to undertake anything and venture anything, they would never have found people to be employed. And then the bodies of the dead would have lain above ground, and have perished and rotted in a dreadful manner.

But the magistrates cannot be enough commended in this, that they kept such good order for the burying of the dead, that as fast as any of these they employed to carry off and bury the dead fell sick or died, as was many times the case, they immediately supplied the places with others, which, by reason of the great number of poor that was left out of business, as above, was not hard to do. This occasioned, that notwithstanding the infinite number of people which died and were sick, almost all together, yet they were always cleared away and carried off every night, so that it was never to be said of London that the living were not able to bury the dead.

The Diseases and Casualties this Week.

Abortive	4
Aged	45
Bleeding	1
Broken legge	1
Broke her foull by a fall in the ſtreet at St. Mary VVool-church-	1
Childbed	28
Chriſomes	9
Conſumption	126
Convulſion	89
Cough	1
Dropſie	53
Feaver	348
Flox and Small-pox	11
Flux	1
Frighted	2
Gowt	1
Grief	3
Griping in the Guts	79
Head-mould-ſhot	1
Jaundies	7

Impoſthume	8
Infants	22
Kingſevil	4
Lecuargy	1
Livergrown	1
Meagrome	1
Palſie	1
Plague	4237
Purples	2
Quinſie	5
Rackets	23
Riſing of the Lights	18
Rupture	1
Scurvy	3
Shingles	1
Spotted Feaver	166
Stilborn	4
Stone	2
Stopping of the ſtomach	17
Strangury	3
Suddenly	2
Surfeit	74
Teeth	111
Thruſh	6
Tiſſick	9
Ulcer	1
Vomiting	10
Winde	4
Wormes	20

Chriſtned	Males	90		Buried	Males	2777		
	Females	81			Females	2791	Plague-	4237
	In all	171			In all	5568		

Increaſed in the Burials this Week ———— 249

Pariſhes clear of the Plague———— 27   Pariſhes Infected ———— 103

The Aſſize of Bread ſet forth by Order of the Lord Maior and Court of Aldermen,
A penny Wheaten Loaf to contain Nine Ounces and a half, and three
half-penny White Loaves the like weight.

Fig 10.0 A Bill of Mortality in London for the week 15—22 August, 1665.

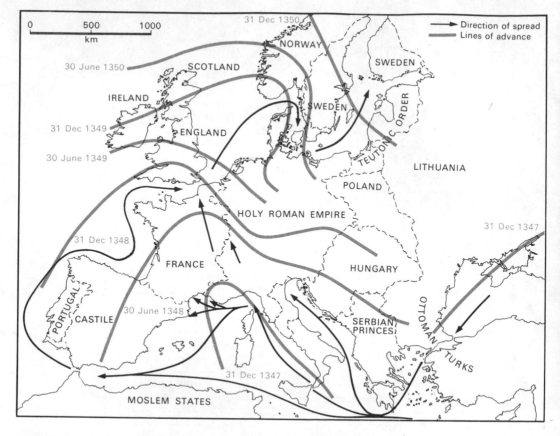

Fig 10.1 The spread of the Black Death, 1347–1350.

Map labels:
0 500 1000 km
31 Dec 1350
Direction of spread
Lines of advance
NORWAY
SWEDEN
30 June 1350
SCOTLAND
IRELAND
SWEDEN
TEUTONIC ORDER
31 Dec 1349
ENGLAND
LITHUANIA
30 June 1349
POLAND
HOLY ROMAN EMPIRE
31 Dec 1347
31 Dec 1348
FRANCE
HUNGARY
PORTUGAL
CASTILE
30 June 1348
SERBIAN PRINCES
OTTOMAN TURKS
31 Dec 1347
MOSLEM STATES

Black Death

In the middle of the fourteenth century a devastating plague spread northwards through Europe, killing twenty million people — one quarter of Europe's population. Although plague is still present in parts of Asia and Africa, we find it difficult to imagine the terror people experienced.

The origin of this outbreak of *bubonic* plague has been traced to the East in the early fourteenth century. It caused great havoc in China. The Chinese actually used the plague as a weapon against their enemies, by catapulting infected bodies into foreign villages and cities. This method, and natural spread, allowed the disease to spread through China. From parts of China and other Eastern countries, ships carried the plague to the Mediterranean. The first European state to suffer the effects of the disease was Italy. From there it spread to Spain, France, Britain, Central Europe and Scandinavia.

The plague was transmitted to man from fleas which were carried by black rats, ground squirrels and other rodents. Some people believed that the black rat was introduced into Europe during the Crusades by expeditions returning from the Middle East.

The greatest encouragement to the spread of disease came from the overcrowded villages and unsanitary conditions. With no knowledge of any other way of life, the people could do nothing but watch the disease spread. Each year the epidemic reached a peak in the late summer when the fleas were abundant. During winter there was a quietening in activity but the fleas renewed their attacks with the arrival of spring.

Victims of the disease died after 2 to 6 days. During this time there was agonizing pain, high fever, prostration, boils, carbuncles and blood-spewing. Dark blotches over the skin were a sign to other people of the victim's plight, and gave the plague its local name of 'Black Death'.

People fled from their homes, villages, wives, children and neighbours at the approach of the plague, but in many cases they escaped only temporarily. The wealthy nobility tried to isolate themselves in castles and manor-houses but to no avail. Cemeteries were greatly enlarged, but they were frequently run by criminals who charged large sums of money because of the risk of infection. Bodies were then thrown over town walls in cartloads. Crime increased with the breakdown of social patterns, and looting of the possessions of dead and dying people was common.

Many long term effects were also felt. Food was short throughout the plague, and afterwards, because there was not enough labour to work or supervise the farms. Commerce and business slumped. Schools and universities were closed because of lack of qualified people to run them.

Historians also cite the Plague as a cause of the increase in social unrest and peasants' uprisings, and the increase in strange cults, Satan worship and a morbid fascination in the grotesque. However there was also an increase of concern about sanitary conditions in towns and cities. The fright and horror of the Black Death was handed by personal stories to subsequent generations, and by literature and art to the present day.

■ DISCUSSION

1 What were some of the dangers to health which allowed the disease to spread?
2 What was the reaction of the people to the insidious spread of the plague?
3 Read the stories of Chaucer and Boccaccio which deal with people and plague.

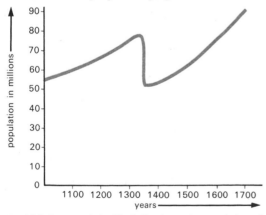

Fig 10.2 Impact of the Black Death on the population of Europe.

Foot - and - mouth disease

Foot-and-mouth disease is a highly infectious disease of cattle, pigs, sheep and goats. It is significant to city-dwellers as well as stock-owners, for two reasons. First, it spreads very quickly, and is a very debilitating disease. Although it kills less than 5 per cent of infected animals it causes rapid weight losses and marked drops in milk production. Second, the effect of a rapid spread of this disease on a nation's economy would be very serious, for obvious reasons.

England and Wales have had outbreaks of the disease at various times, and areas of South-East Asia have had serious and long-lasting spreads of the disease. Because the disease spreads very rapidly, many countries have a strict checking system for the entry of animals and people from overseas. Australia demands that a person entering the country declares any agricultural produce, and any visits to a farm, abattoirs or meatpacking establishment.

If an outbreak does occur, the procedure in Britain and Australia is to close the affected area and try to contain the outbreak. People, vehicles and goods entering or leaving the area are disinfected. Animals suffering from the disease are killed in a 'slaughter-out policy' in order to completely eradicate the disease.

A stock-owner can recognize early signs of the disease by the appearance of blisters on the tongue, lips and feet of animals. The blisters soon rupture leaving painful areas which may cause lameness. The disease is caused by a virus which can spread rapidly within a herd. The virus can also be carried by man or vehicles, on hair, wool, leather, rubber or animal fodder. It is destroyed by boiling or using disinfectants such as formalin and caustic soda.

The State Health Departments of Australia work to prevent an outbreak of foot-and-mouth disease by operating strict quarantine controls and by educating stock-owners in the methods of early detection and eradication.

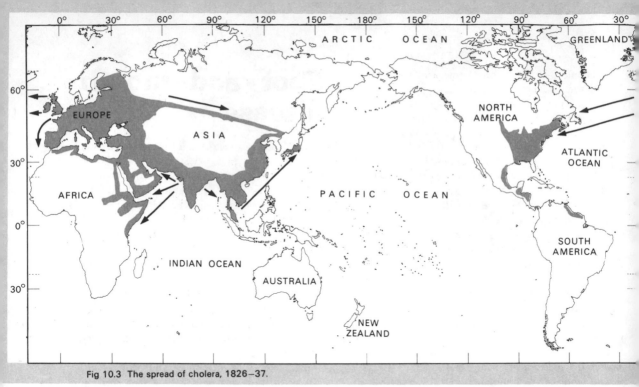

Fig 10.3 The spread of cholera, 1826–37.

Cholera

Cholera is a very infectious disease, which causes sudden vomiting, dehydration, diarrhoea and death. It is *endemic* to parts of India — this means that it is of continuous occurrence in these areas. During the early nineteenth century it spread to south-east and eastern Asia and westwards to Europe and North America. The cholera *epidemic* (prevalence of the disease for a period of time) spread and later retreated across Europe. Outbreaks occurred in Leeds in 1832 (700 deaths), Cardiff in 1849 (400 deaths), and Merthyr Tydfil in 1849 (1400 deaths).

The causes of the spread of cholera were only guessed at by most doctors. They observed the correlation of the disease with slum areas of poor drainage and sewerage but did not know the reason. However, in an outbreak of 1854 in the Soho district of London, Dr John Snow mapped the distribution of deaths from cholera (fig 10.4). He found that they centred around a particular area and were not randomly distributed. The 'cholera field' as Snow called it was centred on a water pump in Broad Street. Within the small area of the field, over 500 people died from cholera in ten days of September 1854.

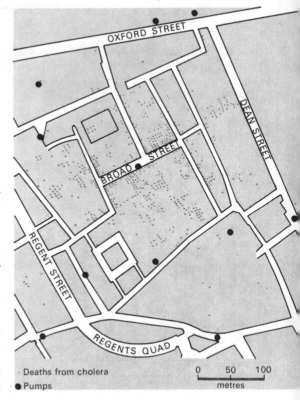

Deaths from cholera
● Pumps

0   50   100
metres

Fig 10.4 Map based on the original by Dr John Snow, 1855 indicating the Broad Street pump as the source of infection.

Dr Snow noticed the correlation of the 'cholera field' with the location of the water pump, and also the fact that a cholera victim who lived at a distance had had her water brought from the pump. He asked an engineer to examine the well. It was found that the water had become contaminated by seepage from a leaking cesspool. Snow removed the handle of the pump, and the epidemic declined in that area. Contaminated water was thus found to be a means of spreading cholera.

Although cholera continued to spread for twenty years, knowledge of the role of contaminated water led to gradual control. Quarantine and inoculation have restricted the disease to its endemic area in India until 1961. A new strain of cholera (known as 'El Tor') then spread from Sulawesi in Indonesia to thirty countries in Asia, Africa and Europe. Research on vaccines and control is continuing.

■ ACTIVITY

1 What other diseases are endemic to particular areas? Look at information and maps of the distribution of leprosy, yellow fever, sleeping sickness, smallpox, malaria, influenza, polio and encephalitis.
2 Collect newspaper reports of the outbreak of a disease in a particular area. Compare the location of outbreak with the area where the disease is endemic.

Locusts

The Bible describes the locust plague in Egypt in the time of Moses, about 3400 years ago. Plagues have continued to occur through many regions of the world to the present day.

In Africa, Eastern Europe and South-East Asia, the migratory locust (*Locusta migratoria*) is a serious pest. The name *locust* is given to grass-hoppers which have the habit of forming dense swarms and migrating in these swarms.

In Australia, the most destructive grasshopper is the Australian plague locust (*Chortoicetes terminifera*). The adult locust has a body about 25 mm long and a wingspan of 60 mm. A black

Fig 10.5 Locust plague in East Africa. (Photo: Paul Popper Ltd)

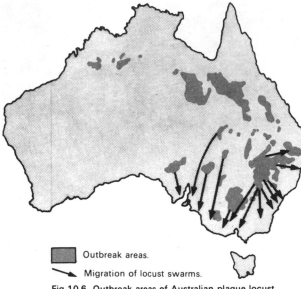

Outbreak areas.

Migration of locust swarms.

Fig 10.6 Outbreak areas of Australian plague locust.

There has been a great deal of research into control of locust plagues. There is a Locust Patrol Service in N.S.W. which continually assesses the populations of breeding grounds. When an outbreak does occur, the swarms of locusts can be sprayed, but this is very expensive. Research suggests that the population can be reduced in breeding areas by allowing sheep to graze heavily on pastures or by replanting areas of trees. Experiments are also being conducted by the C.S.I.R.O. with a small parasite wasp (*Scelio fulgidus*). This wasp can completely destroy the egg-beds of locusts. If it is released in large numbers at strategic times it may be an effective agent of control.

The research on the Australian Plague Locust has been encouraged by the Anti-Locust Research Centre in London. It is hoped that information gained about different locust species will be able to be applied to other parts of the world. Many of the habits of locusts in other areas are similar to those in Australia, including the life-cycle and the migrations from breeding grounds. One year of destruction of crops by locusts in Africa or Asia may mean famine and death for thousands.

tip on the hind-wing distinguishes it from other grasshoppers.

Plagues of locusts are triggered by wet summers in the inland areas of eastern Australia. Central N.S.W. in particular has been the area of origin of many outbreaks. Recent serious outbreaks have occurred in 1972 and 1974.

In a period of above average rainfall the locusts mate and lay eggs. The eggs hatch only in moist conditions. If the weather becomes dry, the eggs can stay in a state of arrested development for up to a year. When wet conditions continue, the eggs hatch and the adults mate and lay eggs again. The hoppers hatching from the eggs develop into sexually immature adults which fly individually or in loose swarms spreading over large areas.

The continuation of wet weather allows the locusts to reproduce further, adding greatly to the numbers. An outbreak may then occur when there is an onset of dry conditions, and the swarm spreads to other areas. This is the time of greatest damage to crops.

In their breeding grounds the locusts usually feed on natural vegetation, but as they migrate they move into agricultural areas. Wheat and oat crops, irrigated pasture land, and even orchards and gardens can be destroyed by locust swarms. The migration paths of some locust outbreaks are shown in fig 10.6.

■ ACTIVITY

1 Draw a diagram to show the development of a locust plague and its spread. Use the information above and the following facts about the Australian Plague Locust.
a) Females lay eggs about 12 days after mating
b) A female lays about 30 eggs in one pod
c) A female may mate and lay 2 to 4 egg pods before dying
d) Eggs hatch in about 17 days
e) Hoppers hatched from the eggs develop into adults in about 5 weeks
f) Adults mature sexually only in wet conditions
g) A swarm of locusts can move at about 10 km/h
2 Insecticides and sprays are mentioned as means of controlling plagues of locusts. Are there dangers in the use of large quantities of insecticides? You may find discussions in books and magazines of man-made disasters caused by the use of insecticides in certain areas.

Fig 10.7 The culprit in person. (Photo: B.H.P.)

Irish potato famine

Potatoes were introduced to Europe from South America in the sixteenth and seventeenth centuries. In most of Europe by the nineteenth century the potato was grown as an additional food source with the basic grain crops. However, in Ireland there was a unique set of historical circumstances.

Ireland was ruled by the English, and most of the land was owned by absentee English landlords. They sublet it to agents who subdivided it further. Three million farm labourers had less than 0.1 hectare each on which to grow food for their families. All of this area, except the space for a tiny mud cottage, was given over to potatoes. Two-thirds of a labourer's annual income of seven pounds went for the rent of his land and cottage. Potatoes could be planted thickly in the ground, and could be left there until there were needed. They contained enough carbohydrates, protein and vitamins to keep a family alive.

Day after day the peasants dug potatoes, until the summer of 1845. Then, in one month, potato plants all over Europe sickened and rotted. For the Irish peasants, with their complete reliance on the potato crop, it was disastrous. In many areas, all potatoes were destroyed. Peasants and their families were forced to scavenge for nuts, berries, leaves, eels, seaweed and any other edible things.

The cause of the potato blight was only guessed at. People blamed the cold weather and rains, weak potatoes, the Devil, the new locomotives, and the wrath of God. It was the Reverend Dr Berkeley, a collector of fungi, who discovered a fungus on the potatoes, but the proof of its effects on potatoes was not supplied until 1861.

In that year, De Bary, a German, carried out experiments which demonstrated the effects of dusting potatoes with spores of the fungus. Potatoes dusted with spores rapidly rotted and died while others subjected to the same conditions of cold and humidity lived. The fungus was shown to be a parasite. It was named *Phytophthora infestans* which means 'the terrible plant destroyer'. De Bary found that the infection spread by the carrying of tiny spores in the wind. Millions of spores were carried onto other potato plants, there to anchor

Fig 10.8 January 1847: a funeral at Skibbereen in Ireland.
(Photo: Radio Times Hulton Picture Library)

themselves by sending out tiny threads. These threads divided and penetrated through the plant, draining the living cells of moisture, and finally killed the plant. New spores were produced very quickly and were spread rapidly by wet windy weather. Thus most of Ireland was affected within one month of the early outbreaks.

The English Government tried to help the Irish people by bringing in corn and providing relief work and loans. This was one of the first relief programs by a national government. Until that time it had been seen as the responsibility of local parishes. The government aid helped the people withstand the winter of 1845–46, and there was hope that the 1846 crop would be good.

However, in June the rains came again, the blight spread, and by July there were few sound potatoes in Ireland. Government relief measures could not cope. Famine became widespread, and with it came dysentery, typhus and fever. Disease spread quickly in the workhouses full of people forced from the land. The population of 8 million in 1845 dropped by 3 million in 10 years. One million died and two million emigrated to the United States, Canada and parts of the British Empire. The emigrants at first created problems in their new countries, carrying disease with them and crowding together in the slums of cities. However, they eventually had a major influence on the economy and politics of North America as they spread westward, working in the new industries, spreading Roman Catholicism and becoming an important political force.

In Ireland the suffering of the people from famine and disease continued for a number of years. Blight struck again in 1872 and 1879, but discoveries of the preventive effects of copper sulphate dust were beginning to have an effect. By 1890 a defence against *Phytophthora infestans* was well known, but there have still been occasional outbreaks of the blight during this century.

■ ACTIVITY

1 Find out about fungi, their life-cycle, and the spread of spores. Find diagrams or micro-photographs of them.

2 Research in history books on Ireland and the U.S.A. may reveal other influences of the potato famine. Try to find stories or paintings based on the famine and the emigration.

3 What were *workhouses* in the nineteenth century?

11 DISASTERS IN GENERAL

Perception of natural hazards

What are *hazards*? What is *perception*? Every individual sees or *perceives* the world around him in a different way. Your background, your age, your occupation, your experience and many other things influence your perception. For example, some people see the interior of Australia as a harsh or dead or frightening place while others enjoy its space and its contrasts. They perceive the same place in very different ways.

Natural hazards are the risks of danger due to *natural disasters*. For example, a person may live in a forested area for many years with a constant hazard of bushfire but never experience a disastrous fire.

A question which has occurred in a number of places throughout this book is: why do people live in areas prone to natural disaster? In most areas of hazard, the risks are known but people continue to live there. Their reasons might be the need to use highly productive volcanic or alluvial soils, or the desire to live in bushland area, or in many cases the lack of land elsewhere for them to make a living. Much of Japan has an earthquake hazard and much of Australia has a drought hazard, but people who live there do not perceive these hazards as serious enough to prevent them living there.

The perception of natural hazards by most people involves the weighing of the attractions of an area against its hazards. Of course this is based on the individual's knowledge of the natural hazards, which may be incomplete. Furthermore, people often forget events of the past, or their memory distorts them. A natural disaster which has occurred once in the last thirty years in a particular area is unlikely to be perceived as a great hazard by most people. Even a hazard which occurs annually, such as tropical cyclones, may be disregarded or accepted as a part of normal life.

■ ACTIVITY

Try to discover how people in your area perceive natural hazards.

1 Firstly draw up a list of any natural disasters, however minor, which have affected the area. Even if you live in a city which has never had an earthquake or a tropical cyclone, you will probably find that either drought or flood has affected the area at one time or another.

2 Devise some questions which will assess a person's perception of these hazards. Possible questions are:

• Can you remember any occurrences of (name the hazard) in this area?

• In what years were they most damaging or serious?

• Does the future risk seem to you

a) very high?

b) medium?

c) very low?

Fig 11.0 Hazards in unexpected places: flash flood in Elizabeth Street, Melbourne. (Photo: The Age).

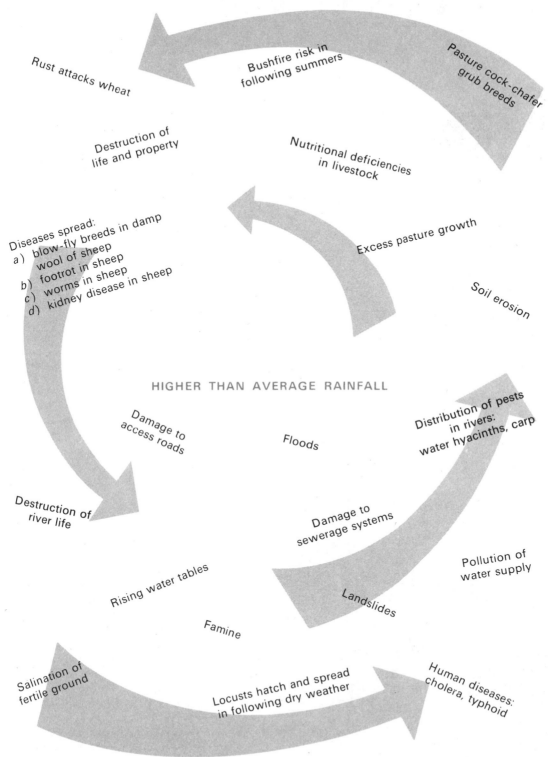

Rust attacks wheat

Bushfire risk in following summers

Pasture cock-chafer grub breeds

Destruction of life and property

Nutritional deficiencies in livestock

Diseases spread:
a) blow-fly breeds in damp wool of sheep
b) footrot in sheep
c) worms in sheep
d) kidney disease in sheep

Excess pasture growth

Soil erosion

HIGHER THAN AVERAGE RAINFALL

Damage to access roads

Floods

Distribution of pests in rivers: water hyacinths, carp

Destruction of river life

Damage to sewerage systems

Pollution of water supply

Rising water tables

Landslides

Famine

Salination of fertile ground

Locusts hatch and spread in following dry weather

Human diseases: cholera, typhoid

Fig 11.1 The direct and indirect effects of a single environmental change: above average rainfall can be destructive in a variety of ways.

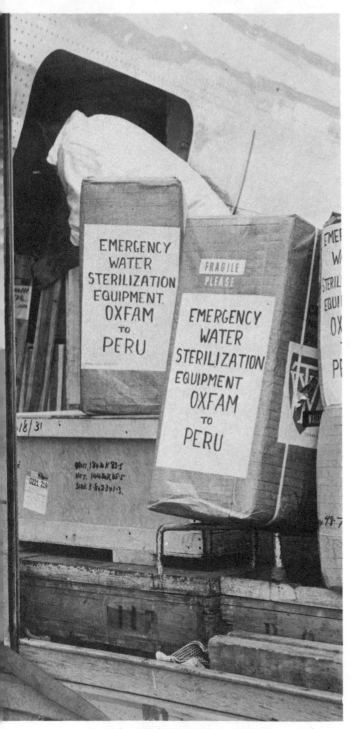

Fig 11.2 Vital following almost any natural disaster — water sterilization equipment. (Photo: OXFAM & Brenard Photographic Service)

● Have you ever considered moving to another area because of the risk?

● What factors are more important than the risk, in determining where you live?

3 Devise a corresponding set of questions asking people about their perception of the hazards in other areas. Again, the questions should attempt to discover what actual knowledge the person has of disasters, and how they perceive the risks. The questionnaire should be given to a variety of people so that information is as representative as possible.

4 Set out the results of both sets of questions in a table or graph. Make sure you have obtained accurate accounts of the disasters in the areas referred to. Compare these with the results of the questionnaires and discuss the differences and discrepancies.

Emergency relief operations

Immediately after a disaster the first provisions to the victims should be:
● food
● clothing
● medical and hospital care
● shelter
● rehabilitation and welfare

This is the operating basis of Red Cross relief operations throughout the world.

The American Red Cross advise their regional branches to form Disaster Action Teams which are skilled and equipped to operate in an emergency. The teams have three to six members equipped with first aid materials, blankets, and flashlights. Their functions are to:
● meet the immediate, urgent needs of victims
● make contact with authorities and public officials
● appraise the disaster situation and report to Red Cross headquarters
● determine and report the need for additional Red Cross services

Disaster Action Teams have access to supplies of first aid equipment, cots and blankets, paper cups, and portable thermal food and drink containers.

Simulation - disaster relief

Imagine that you have been delegated to draw up a relief plan for your neighbourhood or district. The plan must be adaptable to a variety of natural disasters. It should be aimed at providing the most suitable help for the people over a period of five days after the disaster strikes.

ACTIVITY

1 Read through the information on disaster relief work and case examples of disasters in this book.
2 List the immediate needs of victims which you must provide for.
3 Decide which buildings or places in your district will be central to relief operations.
4 Decide which people or groups of people will be responsible for providing for victims. Which organizations will help you?
5 Work out the best emergency communication plan to allow messages and information to be exchanged quickly. Why is this important?
6 Where will the food and goods necessary for relief operations come from?
7 What difficulties do you foresee in making your plan operable? Discuss your plan with others, answering and accepting criticism.

Action in Australia

In 1974, the Australian Government decided to create a Natural Disasters Organization. The aim was to absorb the existing Civil Defence Organization and put new emphasis on the threat of floods, bushfires and other disasters. The regular defence forces will also be associated with the N.D.O.

The Government also commenced inquiries, in 1974, into the possibility of wider insurance cover than was available. Insurance cover against drought, particularly, was to be investigated.

A press statement from the Prime Minister said that 'there is evidence enough that ill-planned and over-crowded cities are exposing people to great dangers in times of disaster. It can be anticipated that this Government will look very warily at any future projects that might expose people or the environment to peril'.

Since this has been written, other statements will have been made by the Government. Collect newspaper clippings and information about action on natural disasters taken by the Government.

Fig 11.3 Any disaster may cause disease — emergency medical aid is essential. (Photo: Austcare)

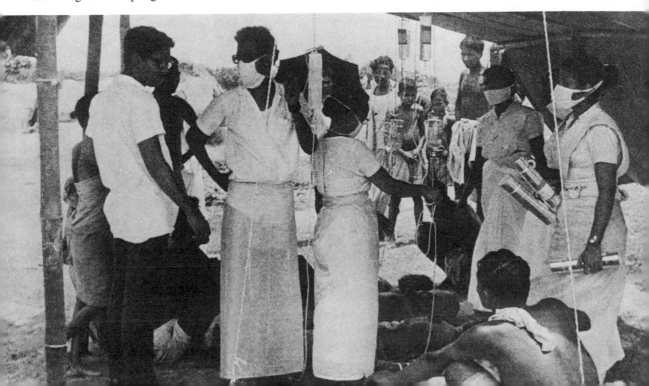

Interview with Mr Alan Werner, National Director, Red Cross Youth

Fig 11.4 Alan Werner.

Mr Werner was involved in Red Cross relief action during the race riots in Kuala Lumpur in 1969 and represented the Society at an international disaster administration seminar in 1972. Subsequently he took up an assignment in Geneva to study the international relief organisation of the Red Cross. During this time he worked as a Desk Officer for the Nicaraguan relief operation.

Q: Have you been to the site of a recent disaster while relief operations were being undertaken?

A: Yes — the most recent one being the Queensland floods where I was the Co-ordinator-in-Chief for the Red Cross Relief operation.

Q: What are some of the things done by the Red Cross in Australia in the field of disaster action?

A: The main fields of operation for the Australian Red Cross are food, shelter, clothing, tracing and enquiry, first-aid, and blood transfusion. The Society works broadly within the Civil Defence organisation.

Q: Do overseas Red Cross Societies undertake different responsibilities?

A: Yes. National Red Cross Societies differ greatly in their work. Although the common bond of Red Cross Societies is relief to the suffering, the kind of relief needed and the resources available are determined by the kind of disaster likely to occur in a given area e.g. in Indonesia the Red Cross young members are very effectively trained in Search and Rescue operations — they have accepted this responsibility as at present no other organisation is in this field. In Canada, members carry out rescue operations in the snow-fields. Austria has problems of missing mountain-climbers and a team of men and tracker dogs are on constant search and rescue operation duty. The American and Canadian Red Cross Societies are responsible for the Water Safety programmes in their respective countries and they train the instructors, lifesavers and swimming instructors.

Q: What other organisations in Australia are involved in natural disaster relief?

A: State Governments — finance, transport. Federal Government—finance, manpower (Armed Services). Red Cross, Civil Defence, St. John Ambulance, State Fire Authorities, Police, Church organisations, Service Clubs, etc. Suffice to say that the local community resources are utilised but mainly to augment the major organisations which are charged with the responsibility of relief in time of Emergency.

Q: Are there any particular steps which Red Cross would like to see the Australian Government take regarding natural disasters?

A: The Australian Government has recently established a Natural Disasters Organisation which will co-ordinate the activities of the State Emergency Organisations and will provide the necessary back-up services to enable prompt relief action to be taken, however big the disaster may be. The statutory responsibility for control of relief operations rests with the States, but there are occasions, as in the recent Queensland experience, when the State facilities were inadequate and close liaison between Federal, State and Local Governments was lacking. Disaster relief must be handled on a national basis and must be able to enlist the support and active involvement of all the community resources already in existence.

The Australian Government's new Disaster Organisation represents a positive step in this direction. Eventually it is hoped that prevention of disasters and the various activities associated with it will come within the scope of the Natural Disaster Organisation.

Q: In your experience of the Brisbane floods, or other disasters, what are the greatest immediate problems for the people affected?

A: A state of euphoria, shock, drama, and panic do not help to bring order out of chaos. One of the major functions of a relief worker is to bring about calm and be confident about being able to cope with the situation and to reassure those affected that they have help and assistance and that the danger is over, if it is, or that they will be got to a safety area.

One of Brisbane's major problems was the drama introduced into the scene by disc jockeys, the press, television, politicians and overtired voluntary workers. Relief workers also have to be told by an authoritative person when to take time off; the authority for co-ordinating the Brisbane relief operation was negligible and as a result many people were staying at their posts stirred on by a sense of duty, but because they had been there for many hours many of them had become ineffective and a problem to other workers.

Families which have become separated will not be effective either in keeping themselves or anyone else until they know the whereabouts of missing relatives and loved ones.

Food and clothing supplies usually are a requirement facing authorities after a disaster. In Brisbane food was getting through but organisations did not know what their respective organisations' capabilities were and there was duplication in some areas whilst in others people suffered through lack of adequate supplies of essential goods.

Housing is a major problem. If families are billeted it means the breakup of family groups and for a family that has lost everything this is a traumatic experience.

Q: What are the greatest long-term problems?

A: Rehabilitation — the younger a person or family is, the more able they are, usually, to make a fresh start. But older people often see a major disaster as the absolute end for them. Their ability to cope is greatly affected by their lack of energy or health.

There are a remarkable number of legal and financial hurdles to overcome — legal papers lost, receipts lost, etc. In the Queensland situation most people were not insured against their loss. Many people were building or buying their homes in some cases, their homes have disappeared 'down the river'. They are still in debt and will need to borrow money to build again — an almost impossible task.

Q: Have there been particular relief operations after certain natural disasters which have been very successful?

A: In the long term, my answer is 'yes'. The bushfires in Tasmania caught the population at first with their pants down, as it were, but quick action by many saved property and more importantly, lives.

If one considers the Tasmanian and Queensland situation and the result of those two experiences which has produced a much more aware and organised community to deal with similar situations in the future, we must say 'yes' to the question. However, my answer has yet to be tested.

Q: Almost every area of Australia has some natural hazard for the population. What should the ordinary citizen do as a general precaution against disaster?

A: Know the local authority which deals with such emergencies. Have a basic knowledge of preventive measures. Support, in person or financially, local organisations whose task it is to give relief and take preventive measures. Lobby to make sure that as many preventive measures as possible have been carried out. People should study their own area, be aware of the most likely disaster to occur in the area and understand what he or she can personally do to relieve the situation should it arise.

Research in Japan

In 1963, Japan established a National Research Centre for Disaster Prevention. The aim was to research the physical reasons for all kinds of natural disasters, using laboratory experiments and field data.

A statement from the Disaster Research Laboratory says that it is 'making studies of the theories of disaster prevention, geographic consideration of disasters, the history of disasters, and structural discussion of disasters'.

Here is a list and brief description of some of the work being done:

1 study of the damage to agricultural crops from cool summers and drought.

2 the relation of the collapse of granite rocks to the state of weathering.

3 investigation of the topographical and geological features of sample areas of mountainous country.

4 test-boring into layers of the Matsushiro Earthquake Zone.

5 testing prefabricated houses on a 'shaker table' for the results of vibration.

6 measurements on wind waves in the sea — their shapes, transformation and patterns.

7 investigations of typhoon areas — the energy of evaporation, the relation between momentum carried by winds and the turbulence over the sea surface.

8 studies on the development of measuring instruments for snow and ice.

9 improvement of methods of roof snow removal with hot-water sprinkling.

10 engineering studies for the prevention of damage by loads of snow on buildings.

The Research Centre has 57 professional staff (all university-trained) and sub-sections such as the Storm and Flood Laboratory, Climatic Anomaly Laboratory, Landslide Laboratory, Earthquake Laboratory, Coastal Disaster Laboratory, and Snow Disaster Laboratory. Fifty lengthy reports have been released by the Centre.

Fig 11.5 This radio telerecording seismograph uses computers to analyse all data about seismic disturbances. (Photo: Japanese National Research Centre for Disaster Prevention)

■ DISCUSSION

1 Why does Japan have a centre such as this?

2 What are the direct and indirect advantages?

Rebuilding after a disaster

■ **ACTIVITY**
Draw up a table using these headings:
●Locality
●Agent of disaster
●Date
●Effects
●What inhabitants did
●Aftermath

In this table list a number of the examples of disasters referred to in this book.

You will probably find that the wide differences between kinds of disasters, localities and time, mean that the last two columns of the table show a great diversity.

Perhaps the one generalization which can be made is that after a disaster people want to return to the same area. In nearly all cases of partial destruction, people tend to move back into disaster areas as soon as possible. The basic needs of people for shelter and companionship, and the desire to recover possessions are mainly responsible

Fig 11.6 (a) Saada Hotel, Agadir, before earthquake ...
(b) ... and after. (Photos: U.S. Iron & Steel)

for this. These human desires are strong enough to overcome fear of future disaster. Even in areas of total destruction it has taken strong government action to prevent people moving back to the ruins of their houses (e.g. in Agadir and Managua).

Following a disaster there is a period of relief operations. These are emergency provisions at first (see page 130) but the emphasis gradually changes to providing for the future and long-term needs. Governments and civic authorities tend to make the decisions, sometimes in consultation with the people directly involved.

The need to start again after a disaster would seem to be a good opportunity for thoughtful planning. However, the need to act quickly, the desire of displaced people to return to home districts, and lack of money often prevent this. In North Africa there are some small towns which have been shifted and rebuilt after an earthquake. The opportunity for better layout and planning was taken. However, as can be seen from numerous examples in this book, much reconstruction is disorganized. Repairs are made, people move back to the same localities and the same hazards are there. Provisions against future disaster may be made, but after a while the inhabitants perceive the threat of a disaster as less and less significant. Disaster preparations and precautions in areas of hazard may have been forgotten by the time disaster strikes again.

Religion and natural disasters

When man is affected by some powerful force, he naturally regards it with great awe. Even though we can explain in scientific terms the forces of an earthquake, or a river in flood, or a tornado, we are still fascinated by these phenomena and respect their destructive power. To many people in many lands the respect given to natural forces has been so great that they have seen them as divine agents, and in some cases as gods themselves.

Thus Fuji is the sacred mountain of Japan, foremost among the many volcanoes of the land, because of its beautiful, almost perfect cone. Mayon and Gunung Agung are regarded in the same way by the inhabitants around their slopes

in the Philippines and Bali respectively (see page 32). The life-and-death-giving characteristics of volcanoes and their majestic form gave them a central place in local religions. In some ancient mythologies the thunder and lightning of the storm cloud was seen as the result of battles between gods or a physical show of force by a particular god.

Christianity has also seen disasters and natural forces in its own way. The Black Death was interpreted as a divine visitation on the people of Europe, similar to the plagues of Egypt. For other people the Black Death encouraged an interest in Satanic rites and the macabre.

In 1750, the people of London predicted a time of peril after a small earthquake hit the city. They linked this with the Jacobite rebellion of 1745, with a cattle plague which had caused serious loss, and with a scourge of locusts in the rural areas. The Bishop of London pronounced that the earthquakes signified a 'divine warning that the time had come for Londoners to consider their faults'. John Wesley, the founder of the Methodist Church, wrote in 1777 that 'there is no divine visitation which is likely to have so general an influence upon sinners as an earthquake'.

■ DISCUSSION

1 Find other examples of people incorporating local volcanoes, floods and other hazards into their religion.

2 How did the religions of Ancient Greece and Rome and other civilizations account for natural disasters and the forces of the earth and atmosphere?

3 What natural disasters are described in the Bible? Read the descriptions of these and perhaps some of the modern research into their occurrence.

Fig 11.7 Mount Mayon in eruption. (Photo: UPI)

SOME FURTHER REFERENCES

Brisbane Floods, January 1974. Director of Meteorology, Bureau of Meteorology, 1974.

Bushfire Control and Conservation. Australian Conservation Foundation, 1970.

CALDER, NIGEL. *Restless Earth.* British Broadcasting Corporation, 1972.

CAMPBELL, DON. *Drought.* Cheshire, 1968.

CAREFOOT, G.L. & SPROTT, E.R. *Famine on the Wind.* Angus & Robertson, 1969.

CONSTABLE, GEORGE. *The Neanderthals.* Time-Life, 1973.

Cyclone Ada. Director of Meteorology, Bureau of Meteorology, 1970.

DAVIES, A.J. *Chiefly Fine.* Hall's Book Store, 1968.

DAVISON, CHARLES. *Great Earthquakes.* Thomas Murphy, 1936.

DOUGLAS, D.R. & GRAHAM, B.J.T. *The Clare Fire ... An Assessment.* South Australian Department of Agriculture, 1965.

FRASER, COLIN. *The Avalanche Enigma.* John Murray, 1966.

HOWELL, G.M. *Man, Environment and Disease in Britain.* David and Charles, 1972.

HOYT, W.G. & LANGBEIN, W.G. *Floods.* Princeton University Press, 1955.

JEFFRIES, GREG. (ed.) *Volcanoes.* Jonathan Cape (Jackdaw Kit), 1969.

LANE, FRANK W. *The Elements Rage.* David and Charles, 1966.

LUKE, R.H. *Bushfire Control in Australia.* Hodder and Stoughton, 1961.

MACDONALD, GORDON. *Volcanoes.* Prentice Hall, 1972.

Oceanography. Scientific American, 1971.

POWELL, J.M. *The Making of Rural Australia.* Sorrett, 1969.

PRIDEAUX, TOM. *Cro-Magnon Man.* Time-Life, 1973.

SHIELDS, A.J. *Australian Weather.* Jacaranda, 1965.

STAMP, L. DUDLEY. *Some Aspects of Medical Geography.* Oxford University Press, 1964.

STAMP, L. DUDLEY. *The Geography of Life and Death.* Collins, 1964.

THOMAS, G. & MORGAN-WITTS, M. *Earthquake — The Destruction of San Francisco.* Souvenir Press, 1971.

TIDMARSH, SHEILA. *Disaster.* Penguin, 1969.

Waters of the World. Marshall Cavendish Publications, 1970.

WHITE, GILBERT F. (ed.) *Natural Hazards.* Oxford, 1974.

ZARUBA, Q. & MEND, V. *Landslides and their Control.* Academy of Science, Prague, 1969.

Also current and back issues of:

Bureau of Meteorology Publications

Bureau of Mineral Resources Publications

Daily newspapers

National Geographic

Newsweek

Reader's Digest

Rural Research in C.S.I.R.O.

The Geographical Magazine

Time

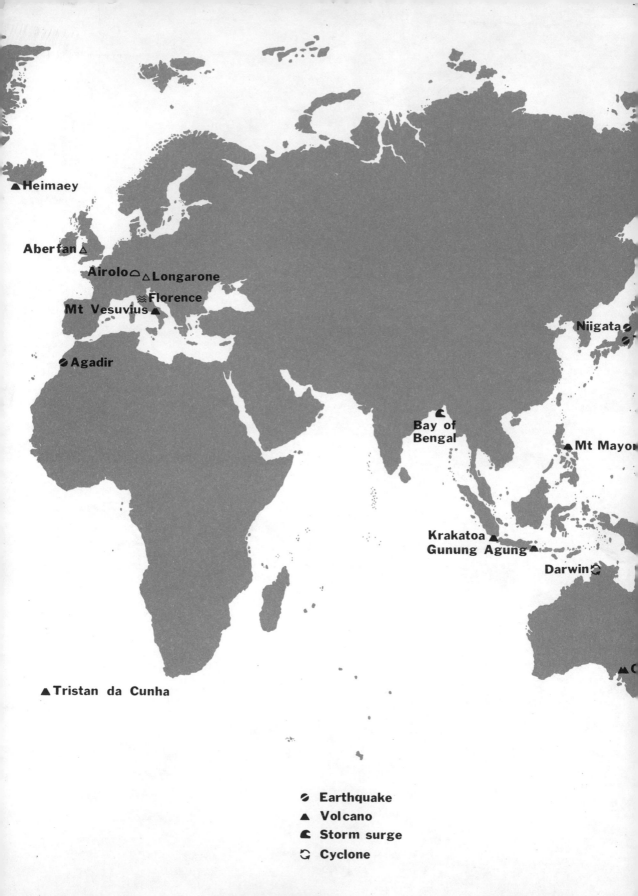

▲Heimaey

Aberfan △

Airolo ◯ △Longarone
≋Florence
Mt Vesuvius ▲

◓Agadir

Bay of
Bengal ◣

Mt Mayo ▲

Niigata ◓

Krakatoa ▲
Gunung Agung ▲

Darwin ◌

▲Tristan da Cunha

◓ Earthquake
▲ Volcano
◣ Storm surge
◌ Cyclone